THEOLOGY for the UNWANTED

THEOLOGY for the UNWANTED

RECLAIMING YOUR PLACE IN GOD'S CHURCH

DANIEL C. TILLSON

Paulist Press
New York / Mahwah, NJ

Cover image by Kluva/Depositphotos.com
Cover design by Sharyn Banks
Book design by Lynn Else

Library of Congress Cataloging-in-Publication Data
Names: Tillson, Daniel author
Title: Theology for the Unwanted: reclaiming your place in God's Church / Daniel Tillson.
Description: Mahwah, NJ: Paulist Press, [2025] | Includes bibliographical references. | Summary: "This book provides LGBT and other Catholics with theological tools of discernment to understand they are loved by God and can live openly"—Provided by publisher.
Identifiers: LCCN 2025015933 (print) | LCCN 2025015934 (ebook) | ISBN 9780809157389 paperback | ISBN 9780809189069 ebook
Subjects: LCSH: Catholic Church—Doctrines | Church work with gay people—Catholic Church | Church and minorities | Sexual minorities—Religious life
Classification: LCC BX1795.H66 T55 2025 (print) | LCC BX1795.H66 (ebook) | DDC 261.8/3576—dc23/eng/20250811
LC record available at https://lccn.loc.gov/2025015933
LC ebook record available at https://lccn.loc.gov/2025015934

ISBN 978-0-8091-5738-9 (paperback)
ISBN 978-0-8091-8906-9 (ebook)

Published by Paulist Press
997 Macarthur Boulevard
Mahwah, NJ 07430
www.paulistpress.com

Printed and bound in the
United States of America

CONTENTS

CONTENTS

PREFACE

To My Fellow Readers in America

FOLLOWING THE TWO World Wars, many of the survivors of Europe saw their livelihoods completely obliterated and their cities lying in ruins. At least 85 million people perished. For those who lived, their hopes and dreams were reduced to a memory. The empires of their ancestors were now just a memory. Such a monumental event prompted massive cultural change, left many people wondering if God is really among us, and for others, it strengthened their faith.

For many of those who continued to believe, that collective experience profoundly changed how they gazed at the crucifix. In some ways, they knew themselves to be imitating the suffering of Jesus nailed to the cross. The pain they experienced transformed their faith from an elite and intellectual exercise to one that was also a *lived experience.*

Theology and sacred tradition become a lot clearer when we allow ourselves to set down our weapons and our defenses. When we take into account the context, audience, and knowledge available to the original readers of the Bible and Church documents, their ancient wisdom suddenly feels like a bright light of knowledge in a dark world. It was only after the Europeans experienced devastation—twice—that they were ready to set down preconceived notions about their enemies, to look at *reality* first, and then see how their thoughts fit.

That is the first step to understanding good theology.

You may think that Catholic theology is a well-prepared defense of the knowledge our grandparents had about the faith. No! Theology is a living and breathing field of study that seeks to understand (International Theological Commission 2011). It is our ongoing work to take an infinite God and explain his designs using our limited vocabulary. Theology is the work of describing reality. It can only become more itself over time, like a plant that unfolds to reveal its true beauty.

The *lived experience* of post–World War II Europe, combined with their many centuries of practice developing theological thought, led to authentic and faithful developments in doctrine that culminated with Vatican II.

This book is written for the Catholic or former Catholic who is suffering immense pain in trying to reconcile who they are and their desire to exist in God's love. If you are like me, several genuinely well-intentioned priests discouraged you from talking about your sexuality and that everything would be okay. At least for me, I don't think it was malice, just an eagerness to end a discussion without taking the time to dive into my experiences or suffering. This book is for you. This is a new day! A day for being authentic before the God who made you! Because theology is reality.

At least abroad, those with doctorate-level degrees in moral theology have started to coalesce around the idea that we are ready for an authentic development in doctrine on the human person—one that is in line with the bounds of sacred scripture and more beautifully explains reality than we previously thought possible.

Going even further, Cardinal Jean-Claude Hollerich, a prominent European theologian, was quoted in Catholic media saying, "I believe it is time for us to make a revision of the basic foundation of the teaching" (Caldwell 2022). This book will explore the criteria and methods that the Church has traditionally used to sharpen, balance out, or mature doctrine. This is something that has been done many times in history.

From Brazil to Europe, for years this understanding has led many bishops and cardinals to either support or allow for blessings of same-sex couples or civil unions without exclusion from Church life. As Swiss bishop Joseph Maria Bonnemain noted, "Every person is unique and is loved by God in his uniqueness." And about those who are gay, "This conviction is increasingly shaping the basic attitude of the Catholic Church" (Michel and Nopper 2022).

As moral theologians across the world have examined the foundations of the current teaching, they have found that the assumptions, one by one, are no longer held as true. But this book is not interested in campaigning for doctrinal development. Instead, you should finish this book and hopefully reflect that you are called to live precisely as God has made you! And that a deeper look at why the Church teaches what it has taught reveals that, yes, there is plenty of room for you to live authentically! To deny a part of how God made you would be inconsistent with the truth.

Our Church is learning and discovering, just as it always has, but in this present moment the individual Catholic's calling is to discern how they were made and to embrace it. But rest assured, the statements from bishops all around the world demonstrate that the overall Church is learning how to be more loving and open to God's diversity in creation.

In early 2023, many French bishops led by Archbishop Giraud reportedly asked the Holy Father to rewrite the three paragraphs of the Catechism dealing with this issue (Tadié 2023). Don't be alarmed; the Catechism is a tool to help everyday Catholics understand a summary of what the Church teaches. It can indeed be edited so long as it reflects what the Church knows of reality.

You may be asking: So how did we get here?

Studies have shown that Catholic theologians and Catholic canonists (church lawyers) began to go their own way, slowly diverging from one another after the seventeenth century. Our understanding of natural law became increasingly expressed as a set of principles and lost its integrated focus on "theological anthropology that considers who the human being is as created…who the being is destined to become" (Keenan 2022, 217). This is partly why the Synod on Synodality (walking together) has been an important project of Pope Francis. We need our lawyers and theologians walking together as one.

We have a ways to go, however. The gap between Catholic professors and Catholic lawyers sometimes feels pretty wide. The President of the Italian Theological Association for the Study of Morals, Fr. Pier Davide Guenzi, says new information has led moral theologians to re-evaluate how we interpret the natural law as it relates to gay people (Moia 2019). And at the same time, those who hold doctorate-level degrees in canon (church) law believe that everything is already as straightforward as it could be.

Following the 2021 declaration about same-sex couples by the Doctrine of the Faith office that "God cannot bless sin," the pope decided to finally restructure that office and remove from office those who helped draft the well-intentioned but harsh document. Although the pope had been thinking of reforms for many years, he ultimately decided to divide it into two sections: doctrine and discipline. In a personal letter to the man he had just appointed, Pope Francis stated the need to move away from an immoral use of the doctrine office as a means to go after those with whom we disagree (Francis 2023).

That doesn't mean we are to throw out the law or lessen the importance of discipline. This book believes both perspectives are validly Catholic, and that the division of opinion means that we have yet to completely understand God's design.

This may seem alarming, particularly if we are accustomed to a simple and easy-to-understand world. But *reality* is more significant than our human limits, and a growing number of theologians and other Cardinals in the Catholic Church are encouraging the *magisterium* (the teaching authority of the Church in union with the pope) to work harder to explain a more authentic theology on human sexuality and family life.

Cardinal Matteo Zuppi stresses that we can reach this without falling into relativism (a term that means the truth is not the same everywhere). He says we need to apply theology according to the concrete needs of particular persons (Moia 2022). We can't exist in a state of nostalgia enforcing the culture of yesterday, but instead must apply reality to the culture today. Cardinal Grech of Malta is convinced the early Church Fathers left us with plenty of wisdom to reach these answers (Grech 2014).

Quite a bit has been said about how significantly different the pastoral and philosophical approaches are between Catholics in America and Europe. When this book uses the term "pastoral," it is less about specific teachings and more about the method we use to follow in the footsteps of Jesus. It's about how we minister to one another.

It's important to realize that in the history of the United States, the Church has at times faced intense anti-Catholicism. You may be unaware of the tensions within the Church if you live here, and maybe that feels refreshing. Strong boundaries helped protect the family and keep us together through some extremely difficult times. Although sometimes in the United States, matters of morality are presented as if they are black and white. This confuses many European theologians, although many of them don't come from a country where Catholics are constantly challenged and prompted for quick decisive answers on what the Church believes.

And yet, I remember that catholicity (universality) is not achieved in uniformity but in unity. So, of course, it makes sense and is perfectly valid that our experiences of religion are entirely different. And so, the Churches of the two continents need one another.

Our ability to grasp theology (reality) will be determined by our *lived experience*, especially our ability to suffer as Jesus did.

We cannot be a faith that occasionally accompanies people who are suffering in the world. Instead, to understand Jesus as he is presented in sacred scriptures, we must open our eyes about every kind of suffering in the world and become a faith that allows us to be informed by it.

There are many reasons you might be reading this book. I cannot promise it will speak to your specific situation. This book draws on my personal observations of differences in how theology is taught, and how it relates to people on the outside. It especially focuses on lesbian, gay, bisexual, transgender (LGBT) Catholics and where the Church may be going in the future.

If you are reading this book, you may have also been told that the affirmation you are seeking is only to dull the pain of your shame.

Many of our Church leaders here grew up during culturally turbulent times, so some of them learned a version of disciplinary Catholicism; which helped keep the family together. Now, however, we must become more mature in our understanding of God. It is not by our own power that we come to live good lives—it is not about the "me." It's about the Holy Spirit helping us to live our responsibilities across the many complexities that life brings about.

And if you have been hurt by a member of the clergy or by their words, take a moment to recognize the worldwide diversity of opinion and pastoral background on this matter. Every priest takes a different approach based on their training and experiences, and so a blanket praise or condemnation of the clergy is not possible.

That is why I hope you will take the time instead to pray through Catholic theology and discern, clearly, the fact you were made in the image of God.

All of this firmly keeps in mind the stern warning of St. Paul, who says we must guard the faith that has been handed to us (1 Tim 6:20–21). And yet, at the same time, the early Church Father and fifth-century saint Vincent de Lérins said "change" is not the problem. "Is there no progress of religion in the Church of Christ? Certainly, there is progress, even exceedingly great progress. For who is so envious of others and hateful toward God as to try to prohibit it?" (Tornielli 2016). How do we recognize the difference?

My hope is this book will help you discern your path to holiness. One that helps you reflect on your *lived experience* to understand your proper place within the Church. Lastly, do not forget the critical role of prayer. Our efforts are unfinished unless we pray before the Eucharist, which transforms us to become more like Jesus.

Come, Holy Spirit! Tear down my walls so that I may love the people of God as the Father created them.

Chapter One

BACKGROUND

THERE IS SO MUCH to be proud of as a Catholic. And yet there are many days when I feel unwanted. Maybe you think that way too. Know that you are not alone. On average, several fellow Catholics reach out to me every month to open up about things they have held tight for so long— it's okay. I have experienced your pain too.

As someone who is conservative and continues to love tradition, it took at least fifteen years to be able to say being "gay" is a God-given gift. I am just one LGBT Catholic, doing my best to search for God, and to share my personal experiences and findings. But I am proudly and definitively Catholic.

More than a few people have scoffed at that, but it's okay. First and foremost, if you have been hurt, I encourage you to give yourself a break. Do not worry about proving yourself to others or figuring out everything in one day. Instead, it is essential that you know this: you are a vital member of this family. Our Church is not complete without you. So it is our Catholic community's collective responsibility to try and do better so that you feel welcome.

Plenty of well-meaning people disagree in the name of not creating confusion. That's human nature. As humans we will always prefer religion that is uncomplicated, has finished discovering the unknown, and serves as a rock in stormy weather. I invite them too to join me in re-learning the rich philosophy and teachings of the Catholic Church, to revisit what it means to encounter God in the Eucharist, and to meditate on the two millennia of philosophy that reveals God is not only loving, but that God is love itself!

The range of catholicity is quite impressive. The Eucharist is celebrated daily in local languages from Syria to Mexico, yet despite our lack of uniformity, we have unity. Our Church history has seen immense change, yet it has all stayed the same in the sense that it is deeply rooted in truth. Not a truth that anyone can possess, but one that we are simply living in. And I believe it to be true.

Some countries, especially those where the population is mixed with a lot of different religions or Protestant traditions like the United States, tend to teach Catholic theology through the lens of discipline. It's incorrect to assume that every priest or every seminary in each area has been taught this way. But if you are reading this book, then maybe you feel that way.

Especially in English-speaking countries, there have been waves of popular anti-Catholicism and so our people have been forced to bond together. That family bond has been important to our survival. Every Catholic family has its challenges and successes, but sometimes we can mistake discipline for faith formation. And it is seldom obvious until you experience the Catholic Church in another culture and think, "Wow, this is the same place?" But especially in the United States, that strong discipline has helped to keep the family together.

However, this has gone to the extreme for far too many suffering individuals. When a Catholic young adult tells me they are now homeless or that their parents no longer invite them to visit, I am moved by the words of Jesus, who said, "They will put you out of the synagogues. Indeed, an hour is coming when those who kill you will think that by doing so they are offering worship to God" (John 16:2). Not every unwanted Catholic has experienced this. Still, we have all been discarded by someone, whether it was a friend or family member. How can we come to understand our place within the Church and maybe one day heal these broken relationships?

Are we to simply throw out the rules? No! But for me, the answers were found through an intense dive into Catholic theology and prayer. The tools are already there. Catholic theology can help you find your place.

An expert of Church law might tell you that sin is simply an offense against the truth, whereas a moral theologian might tell you that sin is nothing more than a failure to love as God made you. Because God is love. In this book, we'll spend more time with moral theology because it explores love of God, and all things and persons whom he created—in his own loving image.

Even the idea of *chastity*, an important virtue in love, has seemingly been altered away from moral theology and demoted to a list of rules that seemingly make it less credible and interesting. When we look at chastity from a disciplinary standpoint, it sounds controlling. But if you put on a theological lens, it's connected to willing the best for your partner and never desiring to possess them. Chastity is a way of presenting love that remedies toxic control in relationships (Francis 2024).

One day, a visiting priest at my parish was available for confessions. The priest is from Italy and also a well-trained moral theologian and bioethicist. Confession is always a risk for people like me. It can either be a healing experience or a harsh reprimand. But that day, I found the courage to walk in and the priest's advice was stunning:

Daniel, I want to remind you that Confession is not a judicial experience even though it may feel that way. You are visiting with a physician of Christ who heals your wounds. And your wounds have nothing to do with being gay or not being gay. Your wounds start with not being able to love yourself fully, as you were created. Maybe you have become biased from the mean things other people have said to you. And that prevents you from fully loving God and others the way you were intended. That is when we start to sin against God. Because we have not loved.

It was a very mature Catholic theological approach. It struck me how differently I viewed the sacrament of reconciliation before that moment. As a child, I viewed Confession as exchanging dirty clothes for clean ones, sort of like visiting the dry cleaners and getting back a freshly cleaned shirt.

I had simply thought of Confession as a way to get rid of my sins, which is not untrue at all. But my old approach made the sacrament too much about my actions instead of those of the Father, who eagerly offers mercy. As an adult, I understand that Confession is much more than that. It is about allowing God to transform me through his mercy so that I am more like him—the summit and source of all authentic love.

In this book, we will explore scriptural contexts, including the rejection Jesus himself experienced. We will learn from how he lovingly and sincerely admonished some of the well-intentioned religious teachers of his day who spread hate against him, "to fulfil the word that is written in their law" (John 15:25). We will look at how Jesus gravitated toward those who were unwanted in houses of prayer and how he made them missionaries.

Not much in the ways of humanity has changed in two thousand years. Human history is marked by the same patterns of social tension and societal development that Jesus knew. He spoke to those truths. That is why the Church's theology feels quite relevant despite the advances in science and technology.

As previously stated, this book is not written for the theologian, the lawyer, or even the Catholic who finds themself doing very well in Christian life. This book is written for people in a bind. The field of Catholic moral theology is built for an imperfect world. Bound by scripture, it explores how we can maximize good and minimize evil by how we shape our lives. More and more, people are finding themselves in situations totally irreconcilable with Catholic law—yet if someone wants to discover Jesus Christ, we have to help them do that. Professor Mauro Bianchi says that moral theology is able to go deeper than simple lists of things to do or things to avoid. Moral theology gives us complex tools contemplate how to concretely imitate the love of Jesus Christ, and to do it successfully without reducing morality to a series of prohibited actions (Bianchi 2014, 1.1–2). And so we will try to explore some possible theological mechanisms that can help you in your discernment.

If your pain is for a different reason, I hope this book can still serve you. This book is an invitation for you to follow Christ in all of the complex realities that make you exactly who you are. No matter how messy you may think life is, the Church is quite capable of accompanying you exactly where you are. This is why our parishes have food banks, diaper drives, clothing closets, listening hours for the lonely, prison visits, and much more.

(Does your parish have programs like these too? These ministries are symptoms of the Holy Spirit working to sanctify the people by uniting them to the suffering of the world, as Jesus did. When we focus on instilling good theology more than we emphasize the discipline, these ministries will already have all the ingredients needed to thrive and grow).

On some levels, the experiences of some LGBT people in the Catholic Church are similar to what many Black Catholics experienced in the twentieth century. Many cities in the United States, especially in the Deep South, continue to have a vibrant Black Catholic culture. The style of music, prayer, liturgy, and way of life felt foreign to most of the American bishops of the time. Clashes between groups during the civil rights movement of the 1960s only heightened tensions.

Then came along Franciscan Sister of Perpetual Adoration, Sister Thea Bowman (1937–1990), who spoke prophetically about how her identities were a gift to the Church. I'm sure many Catholic leaders in her day felt confused. "What gifts? Why are you so different from us?" However, the Black Catholic community's oppressive experiences in the world have led us to a richer theology.

Shortly before her death, Sister Thea Bowman spoke to the Catholic bishops on her own experiences of feeling unwanted in the Church because of her race. She said that she would not check any part of her identity at the door and that when she looked at the global Catholic Church in the newspaper, a lot of people in the pictures looked just like her anyway (Bowman 1989).

Thea Bowman is now a candidate for sainthood. Likewise, I cannot wait until the day that the Catholic Church recognizes you, the reader, for your gifts and the unique talents you bring to this community. And just like Thea Bowman, I am full of hope.

If you're feeling unwanted or struggling with faith, I encourage you to read this book. It is a book of hope, and it is written to help you recognize your loving place within the heart of the Church precisely as you are.

I hope you, too, will find your answers through a deep dive into Catholic theology.

Chapter Two

THE SCRIPTURES

The Rejection at Nazareth

"REMEMBER TO DRINK plenty of water!" the tour guide yelled as our pilgrimage group hauled up a hill on that June morning. The yellow and white Vatican flag ahead stood in contrast to the pale limestone buildings of this crowded Israeli neighborhood. Our college campus ministry group had reached the "Synagogue Church" in the old city. Many believe this is where Jesus gathered as a young man with other Jews to study and pray. This synagogue was historically built at the point of the highest elevation in any town and where Jesus preached his first sermon. We did not care; it was hot, and at least the Sun could not beat down on us once we got inside.

As we sat together on the stone floor, we tried to imagine thirty-year-old Jesus arriving at the synagogue in what he probably hoped would be a welcome homecoming. Some other men sitting there must have remembered him as a boy or were friends with Joseph, and others probably studied sacred scripture with him. Our pilgrimage group was about to reenact the first sermon of Jesus. This would be the moment Jesus unveiled his mission statement to those he grew up with. Without having any clue what I was about to read, I raised my hand, and the tour guide handed me the biblical passage.

> *The Spirit of the Lord is upon me, because he has anointed me to bring good news to the poor. He has sent me to proclaim release to the captives and recovery of sight to the blind, to let the oppressed go free, to proclaim the year of the Lord's favor.* (Luke 4:18–19)

At that moment, the Gospel tells us that those gathered in the synagogue for prayer were unamused by Jesus' preaching. "The eyes of all in the synagogue were fixed on him. Jesus replied, 'Today, this scripture has been fulfilled in your hearing'" (Luke 4:19–20).

The crowd suddenly became less welcoming. Did he just hint at his own divinity? Who was this man, the son of a carpenter, to quote the prophet Isaiah and to declare himself favored by God to bring good news to the poor? Who empowered him to restore sight to the blind? They were so indignant that the crowd tried to run him off the hill.

It's hard to blame the crowd for their ominous mood. These were difficult times for everyone under Roman rule; the Jews were simply trying to keep the religious family together. That meant preserving boundaries and pushing out those who tried to break them. Faithful people were expected to follow a strict code, so they probably wondered if Jesus had forgotten his roots. Not to mention he declared liberty to the captives, and the Roman authorities weren't exactly known for rewarding communities where rebels came from. Jesus' sermon meant danger for the faithful ones.

At the same time, I have to imagine Jesus never dared to call his home synagogue unfaithful. After all, that would have been where Jesus first studied the scriptures. And as a practicing Jew, it is unlikely he wanted to abolish the disciplinary and cultural practices. Instead, he wanted to distinguish discipline and theology. They are different. And for any Catholic who feels boundaries have imprisoned them, I invite you to join me in exploring the richness of Catholic teaching. Jesus wants us to look up as we journey toward him, and not to walk with our heads down as if we're afraid of stumbling.

This story is essential because Jesus also experienced rejection by religious people, even in his home church, which, if you are reading this book, is maybe something you can relate to. Maybe you also come from a strict community that evangelizes (shares the Gospel) only with disciplinary practices or by discouraging risks. But without discarding their good intentions, you can use the tools of scripture and Catholic theology to discern and understand your worth and your place in the Church. In the 2024 biopic *Cabrini*, the resilient and soon-to-be saint Mother Frances Cabrini faced tough questions from Pope Leo XIII about whether the world was ready to see a woman lead an overseas charitable mission. Humoring him about her abilities as a woman, she said, "We can serve our weakness, or we can serve our purpose" (Dell'Anna 2024). Of course, her womanhood is a gift from God and not a disability. Sr. Thea Bowman faced similar difficulties in the United States when she insisted her interviewer follow her example in repeating "Black is beautiful" on national television (Queen Donnelly 1990). In whatever qualities God gave you, there is an experience of beauty that others will interpret as a weakness or a nuisance.

Let us take a moment and acknowledge again that Jesus lovingly empathizes with anyone who has felt like a stranger in their home parish. If you feel totally convinced that statement is true, then congratulations! There is no need to continue reading. But if you need to continue discerning this, bring your prayers before the Eucharist and read this at your own pace.

A Pagan and a Pope

Listen to the way people talk about faith. In some Catholic cultures, especially those that don't have a solid historical link between Rome and their government, you may overhear conversations that can best be described as "boundary-marking." These are the conversations where people say who should be allowed to participate in the sacraments or just generally in parish life. They want their particular vision of church family to be a model *for the others.*

It is fairly common for former Catholics to tell me that they have wanted to pray at Mass or go back to visit, but were unsure if others would stare at them and notice how they were different. It is also reasonably common for regular Mass attendees to tell me they believe the unwanted Catholics should correct their legal status (being divorced, remarried, in a civil union or other relationship) before the doors of the Church open to them again. Sometimes people share these beliefs with the genuine intention of helping the people they refuse to see.

Unfortunately, in most of these *boundary-marking* conversations (when we make it clear that we only want certain types of people around us), it rarely takes thirty seconds before the person's vocabulary begins to hint at their true desires. When we set boundaries, it is often because we want to assert that our way is right or to defend what we have already won. Sometimes it is out of fear that an outsider will create chaos and destroy the family.

Most regrettably, we often reduce that unwanted Catholic to a symbol of a political agenda. All these things are done without looking at the particulars of a person's situation because we have excluded them without accompanying them.

This is not a new phenomenon. It has been happening since the very beginning of Christianity. In the tenth chapter of Acts of the Apostles, a particular story describes how the Holy Spirit has lessons for both sides (both the person holding up the boundaries and the one pushed outside).

Following the resurrection, things were quite difficult for budding Christian communities. There was not exactly a trusting relationship between the Roman army and the apostles. And so, as the story begins, I can imagine the terror on Peter's face as he looks up and sees Roman soldiers at his door.

Probably to his complete surprise, the soldiers weren't there to arrest Peter. You can imagine the relief on his face. But that feeling was perhaps quickly followed by a sense of confusion. "Why are you here?" Their commanding officer Cornelius had sent them because he was interested in meeting Peter. An angel had appeared to the Roman officer and instructed him that God desired him to meet the apostle.

Cornelius was a Roman centurion commanding about eighty soldiers. Considering he was at the head of an auxiliary unit, there is a possibility he was appointed to this prestigious military position by the arrangement of a wealthy family member back home. He was almost undoubtedly pagan, although the description of him as "God-fearing" shows he had reverence or at least familiarity with Jewish customs.

In any case, you can almost laugh at how eager Peter was to address the elephant in the room. Never in a million years did Peter think he would make such a forbidden visit to a pagan. And to make it even more surprising, when he walked into the centurion's guest room, he found an audience of more pagans waiting to meet him.

The apostle declared to the crowd, "You yourselves know that it is unlawful for a Jew to associate with or to visit a Gentile; but God has shown me that I should not call anyone profane or unclean" (Acts 10:28).

Perhaps owing to just how big of a religious violation Peter initially thought this was, he reported that the voice in his vision instructed him three times (Acts 10:16). Maybe it is worth reading the next three lines aloud to yourself. "What God has made clean, you are not to call profane. What God has made clean, you are not to call profane. What God has made clean, you are not to call profane."

You, too, have been made clean.

Peter continues speaking as the Holy Spirit descends upon the Gentiles, prompting Cornelius and his companions to get baptized. This is a moment of spiritual anarchy. The boundaries set by the religious leaders nearly prevented this incredible moment of conversion.

The gift was a two-way street. The pagan Cornelius helped our first pope Peter become a better Christian. This once-forbidden encounter was transformed into a pilgrimage. And so, by the intervention of an angel, we learn that a model Christian community will have its doors wide open—even to the point of scandal—so that the Holy Spirit can work to transform better both the daily Mass-goer and the person with the courage to try.

Twice Unwanted

The story of Cornelius is an inspiring one. But some will be quick to point out that he was a God-fearing man already searching for truth, and that he already had a sense of reverence for the traditions of the Jewish people. That is true. Although from Peter's perspective, he probably would have assumed otherwise had he not gone to meet with Cornelius.

And so, thankfully, the Gospel offers us an even more shocking example of a "forbidden encounter" that led even Jesus' disciples to hold back their criticism in disbelief.

It may not be hard to imagine being unwanted or feeling second-class. Do you sit in the back of the church, or are you someone who has sat in the parking lot but could not find the strength to go inside? Maybe you want to go in, but your last Confession ended in a disaster, or you worry that someone will recognize you: "What will they think when they see me?" My experience of listening to people's stories tells me that none of these are uncommon.

Well, if today you must stay in the church parking lot, in a twist of irony, the Gospel suggests that our Lord may personally step outside looking for you, and then he may try to recruit you as a missionary. Let's spend some time with John chapter 4.

Samaria was the land between Galilee and Judah. The Samaritans were their own people, in conflict with the Israelites for centuries, not to be mistaken for Jews. Everything about them was considered wrong: their way of life, their scriptures, and their thinking; just to reinforce the message, they were sometimes referred to as dogs.

So it is surprising that this biblical scene takes place about twenty-five miles deep into Samaritan territory. The route Jesus was taking involved a lot of personal risks. But in the height of the heat, a dehydrated Jesus stopped and waited for someone with a bucket so he could grab a drink of water from the well.

Nearby an unnamed Samaritan woman hid out, also thirsty, and waited until the coast was clear to collect water from the local well on the outskirts of town. She probably worried about how the other women might ridicule her or call her names for her many failed and potentially unlawful relationships. She was an outcast.

At noon, the hottest point in the day, she went out to the well, and Jesus asked for her help. She was stunned. Her response was, "How is it that you, a Jew, ask a drink of me, a woman of Samaria?" (John 4:9). The woman felt invisible before meeting Jesus. She was unwanted by the Israelites and unwanted by her people. Yet Jesus recognized that she, too, had something to offer.

This is an important lesson that the Church continually needs to remind itself of. Even the most unwanted person has a gift to offer the Church, and Jesus would travel a dangerous twenty-five-mile path through the desert to seek out that person's gift. This is all the evidence we need to understand the Church has the responsibility to go out to the well and wait for that person others think of as the outcast. Yet we as a Church cannot think of anyone as an outcast.

When people today hear this story, the first reaction is often a kneejerk, "But Jesus told her to repent!" Presumably so. But Jesus' instructions for this particular woman to repent is not found in the Gospel, so we must keep reflecting if we want to understand what moral the Gospel of John is trying to convey.

As the story continues, the disciples themselves are said to have refrained from commenting on Jesus' interaction with a Samaritan woman. As Fr. Richard Rohr said, when we were small children, the only tools our parents had were to discipline us and set boundaries. However, as we mature, we can re-evaluate relationships and structures from a place of love (Rohr 2022). Perhaps the faith of the disciples had matured.

When someone has a juvenile faith, establishing boundaries is incredibly essential. Parents often make their toddlers hold their hands while crossing the street. As they mature, kids eventually learn how to look both ways and make safe judgments crossing the road for themselves. In the same way, as we grow out of our disciplinary first phase, Catholic theology is supposed to become the toolset that illuminates the beauty and diversity of God's creation.

This realization that we must mature in our faith is terrifying at first because we can feel untethered from everything we were taught when we were young. The prophet Ezekiel said, "A new heart I will give you, and a new spirit I will put within you; and I will remove from your body the heart of stone and give you a heart of flesh" (Ezek 36:26).

Flesh is weaker than stone, so our unbridled trust in the Holy Spirit guiding the Church allows us to flourish fully. Moral theologian Fr. Diego Puricelli said, "The Holy Spirit helps us to integrate parts of us that we did not welcome, that we judged and stamped under our feet. The Holy Spirit is who enables us to live the high measure of love that Christ has revealed to us" (Puricelli 2023).

And so we arrive at the final lesson that this particular story in the Gospel of John wants the reader to reflect on. The woman who was previously anxious about being ridiculed was transformed by her physical encounter with Jesus and became a missionary. "Many Samaritans from that city believed in him because of the woman's testimony" (John 4:39). When you embrace all that is you, your faith will not only become more authentic, but it will also become contagious.

Chapter Three

THEOLOGY FOR A CHANGING WORLD

THIS CHAPTER IS a brief introduction in how modernization and shifts in culture often nudge Catholic theology and spirituality to go deeper, allowing the same old eternal truths to be communicated in more meaningful ways to the people of today. This is an important subject to think about before getting to the tougher topics like human sexuality. It's an inevitable challenge for every theologian because culture is the medium through which all faith is transmitted.

Many people assume that their specific experience with Catholicism is the norm everywhere else. But if you go to Mass in southern Italy and later that same day in northern Italy, you'll hear completely different biblical readings. It's the same liturgy in the eternal sense, but not in the way a courtroom reporter would think. If Catholicism were the exact same experience everywhere, its relevance to the problems of the world would be shockingly limited. Countless times, I've heard people tell me that it is not Catholicism's job to be relevant. The irony is they always seem to want it to be relevant to them! But our faith is greater and more capable than any one person or their experiences.

And yes, we as Catholics around the world all believe the same things, but we add our perspectives too. And it often takes more work to determine how things are interpreted through a cultural, national, or political lens. Catholicism is a sort of universal unity, not uniformity.

Whatever culture, place, and time you grew up in, that is the foundation for your understanding of the world, language, values, and even religion. When you look back, you can see just how different the religion found in today's world is from our ancestors.

For example, some scholars say the ancient pagans in Rome seemingly did not believe in an afterlife, nor did they care about whether one would exist. Yet religion was everywhere and in everything. This life alone was too consuming to even think of an afterlife—a simple unknown bacteria could descend upon the community any day and destroy it—and so the chief aim of religion may have been a petition to avoid disaster in the current life, including sickness, war, or famine (Ehrman 2024). In a modern context, none of those are particularly compelling reasons for worshipping God. We have doctors to prescribe antibiotics and deliver babies, a military to keep us safe, and we even have grow lights for our houseplants.

Can you imagine how strange it was to recruit new people to Christianity two thousand years ago? To avoid a miserable death, you and your family are ever in search of the most powerful god willing to accept your offering. Imagine how many sacrifices you would make if it could keep your family happy and healthy a bit longer. Finding "truth" or establishing your identity as a worshipper of a certain pagan god was not something you cared about.

And then, someone from this brand-new group called Christianity wants to introduce you to what they claim is a more meaningful divine figure. His name is Jesus. Keep in mind that earlier in the day you offered a sacrifice to a different god asking him to keep your family healthy. But the Christian followers heard Jesus say, "Those who are well have no need of a physician, but those who are sick. Go and learn what this means, 'I desire mercy, not sacrifice.' For I have come to call not the righteous but sinners" (Matt 9:12–13).

Especially considering he died on a crucifix, Jesus does not meet the ancient ideals of a powerful deity who dominates the others. Instead, in every age, the story of Jesus continually breaks the mold of what is considered good, and instead calls us to something deeper. Actually, through his resurrection, Jesus totally shatters the religious model of the time of who is worthy to be worshipped.

At every age, Christian theology has challenged believers and nonbelievers alike in ways fit for their times. The Catholic faith has shown this repeatedly.

Finding Examples for Our Time

There is a quote often attributed to St. Bruno, who founded an important order of monks in the eleventh century: "While the world changes, the cross stands firm." It is a very popular phrase among the people I grew up going to Latin Mass with. I love our traditions, but the world does not seem to care about them. I don't doubt that St. Bruno would be a fierce defender of beautiful liturgies like the Latin Mass. However, supposing either St. Bruno or his early successors came up with the motto it is worth reading into the deep layers that phrase holds.

As an assistant to the bishop of his *diocese* (a regional grouping of local parishes) in France, Bruno witnessed a lot of corruption and likely suffered for speaking out against it. When one of his students became pope, there is little doubt the future saint overheard many conversations about preparing for war against the Turks, whether Christians could allow Muslims to possess certain lands, and what candidates for the papacy other kings were preparing to support for themselves. For this brilliant and humble theologian, Bruno was surrounded by men who cared deeply about the external appearances of the Church.

By founding his new order of monks dedicating their lives to silence and contemplation, St. Bruno made a major contribution for his day and age in reclaiming the cross for religion instead of politics.

Make no mistake. St. Bruno undoubtedly suffered a lot for refusing to perpetuate the version of Christianity that obsesses over wins. To draw closer to the cross he had to leave behind many opportunities in his religious career. The crucifix—which is a mirror of enduring love—cares very little about which side of a camp you choose to fight for. The universal qualities of the love radiating out from the crucifix simply invites all members, on each opposing side of a battle, to wipe themselves clean with the mercy it pours out. Following World War II, we no longer see kings and queens posturing their favorite candidate to become the next pope. However, that human instinct to battle in God's arena has moved to other areas. As a Church, over the past century we have incessantly demanded that certain groups who make the Church impure be pushed out of the fold, not only to assert a form of religious power over the other, but also to make ourselves feel somewhat victimized.

One modern and prominent example is Sister Thea Bowman who addressed the American Catholic Bishops shortly before her death in 1990. Despite widespread progress, the Black culture, way of singing at church and even preferred way of praying was still considered less than ideal by many in "regular" Catholicism. She is a positive example of how changes in widespread culture can be leveraged to make religious communities stronger too. There is something exceptionally powerful—not powerful in the sense that we start waging crusades and counting our wealth—in knowing that there are many other believers just like you. "To be Black and Catholic means to be intensely aware of the changing complexion of the College of Cardinals. I picked up your Catholic newspaper and I saw the picture Church—the World Church— a lot of folk look like me! [laughter]" (Bowman 1989).

Sometimes the new ways of being Christian that the saints introduce to us are not only about welcoming new groups of people, but also about changes to our ways of life.

In their highly recommended lecture series as part of "The Great Courses," Professors Cook and Herzman make the case for how Christianity had to find new ways to show its followers a deeper and more Christian path. They highlight how the thirteenth-century St. Francis of Assisi navigated challenges to Christianity in their modern world, where everyday life and community was becoming increasingly transactional and centered on money. When the priests and bishops of the day wanted to teach people about holiness, there was a tendency to harken back to the days of martyrdom (Herzman and Cook 2013). In a world where everyone is Catholic, and no one is being killed for their faith, that left a lot of people wondering if it was still possible to become holy.

Even St. Francis, who was acutely aware of his calling to holiness, started to recognize that sometimes he would simply donate money to the church as a form of petitioning God (Herzman and Cook 2013). After struggling for quite some time, he discerned a new model of being Christian fit for the modern world. The result was the founding of the Franciscan order of priests, nuns, and laypeople who reject material possessions and serve the poor in the name of Christ. For them, the way to emulate Christ the Crucified is to become Christ the Beggar.

Once again, in our day and age, modern culture appears to be at a crossroads, just as Francis of Assisi attempted to grapple with eight hundred years ago. In a terrifying open to the Catholic philosopher Charles Taylor's book *A Secular Age*, he declares, "Belief in God is no longer axiomatic. There are alternatives" (Taylor 2007, 2). He is essentially saying we can no longer assume that all people will look at the realities happening around them and conclude that there is a God. In the months after the coronavirus pandemic reached the

United States, news headlines blamed governments, political parties, and certain cultures for failing to prevent the virus from spreading. There was a time not that long ago where people would witness a disaster unfolding and ask themselves, "What have we done to invite God's wrath?" Science has replaced these moments of fear and self-reflection.

In the twenty-first century, the newly understood truths found in advanced biology, psychology, medicine, and other sciences grind up against theology. Think back to the earlier example of Jesus' first sermon in the synagogue. He said his calling was to bring glad tidings to the poor and release the prisoners. The people who listened to him became furious.

One of the consequences of modernization is that institutions must grapple with how certain groups were previously excluded (Taylor 2007, 3). Fast forward to today, it is culturally completely acceptable in many areas of the world to be gay. Neither Jesus nor St. Francis of Assisi had a word in their vocabulary to describe that. There was no inkling that an individual—gay or straight—could have a perception of self that explains how they love and relate to others. They only had the vocabulary for acts and behaviors, not identities. They did not have the capability of describing these types of relationships beyond structural (body parts) value.

Just as Sister Thea Bowman came to the realization that an increasing number of Catholics in the world are Black, changes in external culture are allowing more and more gay Catholics to see that there are others like them. As society becomes more open, a skyrocketing number of individuals have reported abuse in a church setting or in a marriage. The crucifix is never a shield for the worldwide Church to avoid looking at the suffering of these people sitting in the pews next to us.

As St. Bruno said, the cross stands firm. Remember, Bruno was humble, unlike the Catholics of his day who attempted to punish their enemies or win back territories for Rome. The cross is not an invitation to resolve differences through disciplinary actions or applying titles (like good Catholic, bad Catholic, divorced and prohibited from communion Catholic). But we do know that the cross remains an invitation to love.

Catholic Discipline Sets the Pace

But Catholic theology is not only capable, it must also find a way of communicating reality in a deeper way that explains the enduring truths of love. That is because theology attempts to enlighten the reality that we live in, not the past.

Catholic discipline is meant to assist the people of God in walking together as one, both in how we express our doctrine and how we act. The mission of the Church is salvation and our disciplines have a role to play in getting the whole flock there. The problem is the disciplinary training our Church provides is woefully unprepared for a world that is developing new ways of communicating and sharing ideas at the pace that it does.

Occasionally, at first glance new scientific revolutions can look like they are posing a great threat to scripture. As Catholics hold firm to the idea that the Bible is true, there is no expectation that science will ever disprove the teachings contained in Sacred Scriptures. One example is evolution.

Until the previous century, there was no satisfactory answer for the creation of Adam and Eve other than the creator placed a fully formed human on this earth. The expanded consciousness gained through biology has called our faith to grow deeper. Christians are now offered a window into the careful, intentional, and vastly creative plan of God for the world. Evolution allows the Christian mind a sense that the divine is truly building us up from nothing. It is so much more profound than thinking a stork delivered a fully formed baby to the Garden of Eden. But can you imagine your child coming home from school in 1950 to tell you that humans descend from tiny tree-dwelling creatures from millions of years ago? Modernism is terrifying.

Pope Pius XII had to apply the brakes. In his encyclical *Humani Generis* in 1950, he tackles the issues of his day that might prevent humankind from finding God, particularly because of human reason alone. He takes a balanced approach and warns the people that if later proven convincingly, evolution would be praiseworthy but would need to be understood in Christian ways (Pius XII 1950). It was a smart decision.

In real life, authenticity takes time to work out.

Perhaps the goal of Catholic discipline is a sort of holy authenticity. You are holy when you become everything the creator made you to be. Therefore, discipline encourages people to represent the reality of faith in the most genuine and informed way possible—and not spread error. On an interpersonal level, the people are encouraged to represent the commitments they make as Christians by living a good life.

Let's explore what Catholic discipline looks like in real life. A priest reminding a couple they should try to work out their problems rather than divorce is an example of a discipline. The discipline is not theology, but it does remind people of the theology that clearly states God united them as one. So far, so good.

Sometimes though, the disciplines don't fully contemplate what the person is experiencing. Have you ever attended Mass in Latin? It is beautiful. At least for me, it draws me deeper into the paschal mystery. Although in recent years I've come to learn that I once opposed more modern practices coming into the liturgy because it was less like mine. And I wanted people to see the value of the Latin Mass (and still do). Then on my first trip to Rome in 2011, I attended a *novus ordo* Mass (the type of Mass that most Catholics experience at their local parish). But it was said in Latin. So I expected it to be the same as my experience back home.

To my complete and total shock, the guitars came out. Guitars at a Latin Mass? Yes. And they were singing in Latin. I wasn't sure how to contemplate that. Was I opposed because it was a guitar? Was I happy because it was in Latin?

Sister Thea Bowman had similar experiences as a Black Catholic from Mississippi. The way she resonated joy and reverence for the Eucharist was neither strictly Black, nor was it the average American Catholic experience. Can you imagine an Irish or Italian immigrant breaking out in songs of praise at the end of the homily?

Sister Thea Bowman watched for years as Catholic leadership wanted to help Black Catholics tame the characteristics of their culture. Speaking of her people, she said, "They've been told that it's not appropriately serious or dignified or solemn or controlled—that the European way is necessarily the better way" (Bowman 1989). She continued that it wasn't only a matter of cultural understanding but prejudices: "They say, 'We lazy'—They say, 'We loud'—they say 'We irresponsible'—they say, 'We lowered the standards.'" In all fairness to Catholic disciplinary practices, that was likely a product of a time and place that we have made significant strides away from. She highlights the difficulty of calling out gatekeeping. Sometimes we discipline Catholics to keep inherently bad ideas away. And other times, it could be out of fear or prejudice.

As someone who loves the traditions of the Church, I can see how so many people are suffering today because of prejudices against the gifts of sexuality that God gave to each of us. It is not simply a matter of recognizing that sexual orientation is a real thing, and that sexuality is not only structural but also relational. It is a matter of not prejudging people. Today, the lack of authentic encounter with gay people prevents the faithful from a complete and holy experience. "They say we have HIV. They say we are promiscuous. They say we can't keep a relationship for more than a few months."

But they ignore and discount the gay Catholic couple at daily Mass. Look around. Look closer. They are not advertising their lives to the congregation out of fear, but most of the parishes I have visited—even in the most conservative of dioceses—have at least one or two.

Authenticity is something that often brings one closer to the suffering of the cross. The suffering brought about by authenticity helps you to become holy if you embrace it. I regret to tell the Catholics I'm trying to encourage in this book that by being open about who you are, and what you have experienced, others will think you are challenging the institution of the Church. Most of the time these attitudes come from a good place. Our priests and bishops naturally want to keep the Catholic family together. Whatever it is that you have suffered through, know that you are in some way imitating the suffering of Jesus on the cross. However, I firmly believe that for any person who holds an attitude of service rooted in prayer, you will find that holiness and authenticity are two sides of the same coin.

I've been asked before if my ideas take any influence from Martin Luther, who drew a sharp distinction in his culturally turbulent time between the law and the Gospel. No! Professor Keenan in his book on the history of ethics outlines how the canon (Church) lawyers and theologians had a sort of divorce from one another after the seventeenth century (Keenan 2022). Both fields continued developing on authentically Catholic paths, but on their own for the centuries after that. My hope is that they continue improving the ways they work together. I think the universal nature of the Catholic Church necessitates that we maintain boundaries, but flexibly, or in the words of philosopher Charles Taylor, "accompany the seekers without shocking the dwellers" (Keane 2023). This is the key to authentically keeping the family together. History shows that Catholicism will always prefer to go deeper into its own mysteries, and that we as Catholics will develop a common understanding of how to walk together as a family. But that takes time.

For the believer, modernism is terrifying not only because it will call into question our long-held explanations and beliefs of the world but because it often challenges our own behaviors. Ask people how they feel about the future and the responses will make you feel anxious. There are a couple of ways that Catholicism can choose to grapple with this. The first temptation is to say everything modern or new is bad. In that case, we should accept our increasing irrelevance to the world. Or Catholics can mirror what St. Francis of Assisi did long ago and insist that the Gospel carries truths capable of speaking to the deepest meanings of reality. Being relevant does not mean being "relativist" (a term that usually means the truth is whatever you want it to be). No, a Catholic relevance is much deeper.

The world is continually going to face new issues. Especially as science helps us to uncover the deeper and greater realities of life. There is no need to fear that as the cross stands firm. There is nothing wrong with the attitude that the Church must be disciplined, provided we are actually open to the Holy Spirit and neither too eager nor closed-minded toward change. I'd prefer the Church take the time to make sure we are unified in answering questions about people and their status within Church membership. As long as we understand that Catholic discipline is meant to keep the people engaged in asking for what they need, and not on the sidelines silently waiting. Let us draw closer to the cross confident that its meaning—and inherent suffering—will uncover for us the deepest meaning of the Father's love.

Putting Theology in a Catholic Context

Thankfully, at least for Catholics, we can appreciate and be supportive of both science and religion. They are complementary fields to one another. But let's start afresh anyway. Let's briefly set down our assumptions about religion and start with a blank canvas. Suppose we understand that God is the source of all that exists. In that case, theologians are like scientists who use reason and words to explain reality instead of telescopes and experiments.

Theology is the study of how to express an infinite reality. However, because of how incredibly vast the existence of God is, our understanding will, in some ways, be limited by our vocabulary, history, and culture. This is why we must continue pursuing it to understand. Theology is one side of the coin; science is the other.

As a former catechist in a parish that teaches the Catholic faith to Italian and American students, I was stunned when I tried to reconcile the two textbooks and found that the same teachings were taught in opposite ways.

> Teaching about faith in an American textbook:
> *Faith = A + B + C.*
>
> Teaching about faith in an Italian textbook:
> *Students are asked to observe and describe the conditions of A, B, and C. When they finish exploring how these ideas interact, the group is introduced to the new term—in this case, faith.*

The American method appeared much more straightforward. This makes sense; after all, Catholics in the United States are often pressed to give quick and digestible defenses of what they believe and why. Still, the Italian textbook explored how conditions interacted with the *ultimate reality* (God). It forced the students to acknowledge that they must keep learning and searching for a more descriptive vocabulary to better describe theological themes.

Using the Italian textbook means that the students will have to wrestle with ideas, and that theology should be taught in groups. Even in learning the basics of the faith, we should be open to surrounding ourselves with people who disagree or are at different starting points. In the same way, an authentic theology is not afraid of crisis.

If you remember that you cannot own or possess the truth, you have nothing to lose. And if the reality we observe reflects fact, it will be true no matter how many times or places we test the hypothesis. But we have additional tools that the scientist does not have: divine revelation and the help of the Church in discerning, which always requires a lot of prayers.

In other words, a crisis of faith is a reminder that we are still alive and an invitation to take a deeper look at our beliefs and how we are called to live. These are all things to prayerfully keep in mind as you consider how theology applies to your lived experience.

Millions of Catholics feel like their situation, or their experiences, conflict with their faith. One of the main reasons for this book is the increasing number of people who find their lives unreconcilable with Church law. In other words, they look at their lives and see no possible fix.

No matter why you may feel it is tough for you to remain Catholic, I hope that you too will find that a deep dive into Catholic theology can offer you solace and validation. I cannot promise that this will make it easy to forgive those who have hurt you, but it should leave you with no doubt of God's immense love for you. And maybe for some others, exploring faithful theology might inspire you to go out and make the world a better place.

Authentic theology is a *lived experience*. Because if we are simply talking about theology in terms of understanding *reality*, then we must also be living it. That's why learning about theology only in a library or a classroom has some limits. At some point, learning about theology requires going out into the streets and meeting with the people we have ignored or pushed away, because even the experiences of the people we may not like contribute to an overall understanding of God's design for us.

Philosopher Charles Taylor says that, for Christian believers in God, it is like a relationship capable of giving and receiving love. But that it is also something that must be "opened up, transformed, brought out of self" (Taylor 2007, 7). We have this innate sense that there is a greater purpose out there that we will never discover simply by looking only within ourselves.

If we try to live as true and faithful to *reality* as we can, particularly in a faith-based context, then developing an authentic spirituality becomes easier too. It's not about throwing away the rules or petitioning God for easier rules. No. This is about helping people orient their lives positively toward God. That's why we must get this right.

Maybe all this book can do is discuss a simple framework for learning about theology. It is impossible to relay all the wisdom the Catholic Church has offered over the centuries, and learning theology is a lifelong experience.

A lot of people like the topic in philosophy known as "natural law." It's not like a law that a bunch of senators passed. It's kind of like a "law" in the sense that you learned Newton's laws of motion in science class. We're just explaining what is happening around us. So the *reality of our faith* is a less scary way of talking about the *natural law*.

When my high school religion teacher first brought up Aquinas and the natural law, I assumed it was a very long list of rules I should feel guilty for breaking. That is not only incorrect, but it is also not a mature way of approaching the faith. Instead, we should be trying to open our eyes so that we can observe God's creation and understand our complementarity with one another.

Compare these two examples below.

> Incorrect usage of the term *natural law*: I drove my car 10 mph over the speed limit, breaking the law and resulting in a ticket.

In this case, breaking the law is an example of human law, not natural law.

> A better example of *natural law*: I was driving on a curvy road, and the only way to see oncoming traffic and safely make it around the corner was to slow down.

Deep in your heart, you knew that going around the turn too fast could harm yourself or others. It has nothing to do with the speed limit set by the local government or the possibility of getting caught by a police officer. Too often, we reduce the Catholic faith to a tripwire, as if there is a clear moral distinction between 10 and 11 mph. On the other hand, generally slowing down and looking for oncoming traffic demonstrates the driver is acting in accord with a sound understanding of reality.

And so, although we are technically free to speed above the limit, true freedom is achieved by acting according to reality. The reality is that driving safely means that the car and the oncoming traffic are more likely to make it to our destinations and live another day.

And theologians are increasingly recognizing that better observations of reality are leading them to reevaluate how we interpret the natural law as it relates to gay people (Moia 2019). We have to get this right, but we also have to do it without campaigning for an agenda.

Theologians have been examining how our definitions and usage of various terms have changed over time. The meaning of a phrase in one century may be understood differently in the next. Professor Keenan says that neither the natural law nor humans are left untouched by the passage of time. We grow, we understand, we reach new capabilities. He says, "Nature is no longer understood as the pure object we engage and examine, as something distant and apart from the human being" and that the reduction of natural law to "unalterable prescriptions" conflicts with what the great philosophers of the High Middle Ages had in mind (Keenan 2010, 174).

A priest once told me that from his perspective sexual orientation is not real, while another priest affirmed that whenever he mentioned sexuality, he meant the way we behave and not the way we feel. There was certainly a time prior to the nineteenth century that thoughts like that were mainstream. But those same statements in today's usage of the terms could only be true if we ignored a lot of evidence.

The bottom line is that the way we have used terms like *gay* or *sexuality* have morphed slowly over the centuries. So if we want to take a realistic look at what Church teaching is actually trying to teach us, we have to make sure we're using words in the context they were intended.

Fr. Aristide Fumagalli, a professor of moral theology at the Archdiocese of Milan's seminary, tracked these changes in his book *L'amore Possibile* (The Possible Love).

For example, a student of the famous philosopher Aristotle (about three hundred years before Jesus was born) would say that what we now call same-sex relations are contrary to nature because one man takes on a passive role, which is reserved for women. It was about actions and gender roles, not identity.

Fr. Fumagalli's research continues to say there was no concept of sexual orientation back then at all, just actions and judgments on particular actions. "Retro-projecting contemporary categories, one could say that the existence of homosexual people was not conceived, but only of heterosexual people who had relations with people of the same sex" (Fumagalli 2020, 34).

Fast forward a thousand years and people begin to think of same-sex relations as a symptom of a defect.

People who identify as gay or lesbian today would have been understood through much of Church history as either a disease or perhaps a preferred type of crime. It would come up in conversations like, "Why do some people steal from the market?" "Why do some people prefer to have relations with others of the same gender?" It was viewed as a way of acting out criminal urges.

It took until about two hundred years ago for people to begin realizing that same-sex relationships are more than just experimental or self-appeasing flings (Fumagalli 2024).

We simply know much more about the complexity of the human person these days.

And as it relates to sexual identity, Fr. Fumagalli says it is now apparent that sexual orientation expresses the natural variations in how people are predisposed to love another, "in no way different from the heterosexual one" (Fumagalli 2020, 43).

Given the new information that we have, it should be apparent that conversion therapy is not only unhelpful, but also cruel. Our calling as Christians is to help people blossom and become the person they were intended by God's design, even in all their peculiarities that we may not fully understand.

Understanding natural law does not have to be complicated because it is already written in your heart. Take the example of a homeless woman named Sylvia, regularly served by the Catholic Community of Sant'Egidio in Washington, D.C. When she is feeling well, she spends much of her day helping other homeless people. "We are truly alive; therefore, we should act like we are living!"

It is rare that Sylvia looks at her own situation and thinks that she is too different, or too poor, or too outside of the box to live her life to the fullest.

Sylvia accidentally found the key to understanding the lived experience of theology. On one hand, Catholic discipline will tell you all of the ways to live or not live your life. On the other hand, Catholic theology reveals how to build a life that is truly alive. It's about an encounter, not a rule book.

Now consider your situation for a moment. Are you an LGBT Catholic? Or maybe you lost a loved one or are separated from your spouse. Perhaps you have struggled to maintain a connection with family members and think about it ahead of every major holiday. Let's not forget that many single adults would like to attend more Church events, but they are marketed for families or recent college graduates and so they feel left out.

Now repeat aloud the words of Sylvia. "We are truly alive; therefore, we should act like we are living!" There is something incredibly transformative about understanding the primary tenet of the Gospel: God is love. God is not just loving but is actually *love* itself. And that you were not only created in the image of God but in an exceptional demonstration of God's creativity and greatness.

The reason this is so important is that when we fail to love ourselves as we were made or try to deny a part of the truth about how God made us, we inevitably fall into sin. We fall into that sin as soon as we stop bothering to love and live life in the fullest and most honest way that we can.

Each of us, in our diversity, is a reflection of that love. We need to have relationships with others and do so in a way that recognizes the complementarity God designed us for.

Authentic Spirituality

Spirituality is about opening our eyes and our lives to God's design. It is about discovering God's will for us.

So many people feel like they have been deprived of this experience because they were hurt by someone. But the reality is, if we can form a proper spirituality in the parish setting, there would be plenty of space in the Catholic Church for everyone.

Consider just how far Jesus Christ went to make himself accessible to the entire world. He is at every Mass celebrated in every country in the world, and he invites the faithful to receive him—so that he can transform you to be more like him. Surely a God that makes this much effort is patiently and excitedly waiting to see you too.

There is a large group in the global Catholic Church called Communion and Liberation—a prominent organization present in many countries around the world and a movement favored by both St. John Paul II and Pope Benedict XVI. It began before Vatican II with the organic efforts of Monsignor Luigi Giussani, a theology professor who recognized that young people couldn't connect with the faith as easily as their grandparents.

He wasn't surprised so much that the new generation could not recite from the teachings of the Church, but that they showed, "a more general and profound ignorance about the nature and essence of Christianity as an event that involves and transforms one's life" (Rondini 2000).

The people of God were just going through the motions. And

so members of Communion and Liberation gather in small groups around the world and reflect on theology, its practical implications, and then go out and perform works of charity.

Sometimes we want the faith to be a simple black-and-white book of answers. Sometimes we just want the priest to tell us yes or no, or we want the priest to give us a checklist of things to do or not do. Sometimes focusing on the rules and boundaries demonstrates that we're not cultivating a *lived faith experience*.

There is a particular story of a visit I made to Rome that finally made it click: prayer and mission always go together. Rome is a chaotic place for a pilgrimage, but the city is also adorned with hundreds of extraordinary, marble-clad churches called basilicas. Despite how alive and crowded the city feels, you get the sense that you are somewhere ancient. You're amused that thousands of Italians can walk past the Colosseum on their way to work without gazing in awe. The culture, crowded buses, and the Italian way of life entertain you. And at the same time, you notice that there are homeless people everywhere.

We are not talking about a small handful of irregularly housed individuals needing care. No, there are up to twenty thousand homeless people living there. Almost all the tourists and locals pass by each of them without even acknowledging their presence. Of course, it's a little overwhelming to think about the scale of the problem. But, on the other hand, what can one person really do? And if you are pressed for time and want to visit a particular church, you may have to step over a sleeping person to get into the building.

None of the homeless people sleeping outside pose any actual threat to you, but you feel awkward. And it continues to be awkward no matter how many times you may have had to politely tiptoe around someone sleeping.

I, too, found myself stepping around a homeless person to make my way into the Basilica of San Carlo al Corso. A priest was sitting at an open table, waiting a very long time for anyone to approach him and ask for the sacrament of Confession. Not taking my own advice, I decided to ask him for a checklist of things a Catholic should do.

As I passed by him on the way out, I said, "Father, I am visiting Rome and am not used to seeing so many homeless people. What is a good Christian supposed to say to them?" To be honest, I thought I was asking something righteous.

Wrong. Little did I know that he was about to flip my entire approach to Christianity.

"Sit down," the priest commanded me in Italian. He continued, "You must remember that each one of these persons is in some way imitating the suffering of Jesus on the cross. Each one of them has a Father in heaven who eagerly desires to see them just as the Father desires to see you. And Mary looks over each of them as if they are her children."

Oof. That was the end of his advice. The priest's words took me aback. I had never thought of the homeless in this way before. But the priest was right. Each of these people was a child of God and deserved to be treated with compassion and respect.

The priest's words have stayed with me ever since. They have helped me see the homeless in a new light and inspired me to reach out to them with love and kindness.

As if the advice wasn't hard-hitting enough, he wrapped up his lecture with, "Now say your act of contrition, and I will forgive you." This implied that he felt my approach to "dealing with" the homeless was sinful.

Of course, the lesson is that in Catholic spirituality, we do not seek to manage the unwanted but instead come to serve them. These moments are like an encounter with the divine. Just as we believe Jesus is physically present in the Eucharist, serving those who have been discarded is like attending a school where Jesus is the teacher.

By the way, those who participate in Communion and Liberation call their weekly gatherings the "School of Community."

In this sense, Catholics need the poor and the unwanted more than they need us. It is never really about the money or food we offer them, but about growing in our ability to see the dignity of every person, including those who are invisible or discarded from society. That priest at San Carlo probably has no idea how he changed my life. I continue to reflect on how important it is to adjust my perspective to how God views those around me with compassion and love.

In the same way, it is all too common to think about ourselves as a human obstacle that people must step over to get into the church. We might desire God to be closer in our lives but are allowing something that seems embarrassing to hinder the relationship. The number of people who have told me they are LGBT but want to keep that hidden from their family and friends is a bit overwhelming. And based on how certain Catholic family members treated me, I certainly do not blame them. The reality is every single parish has LGBT people sitting in the pews, including smaller parishes and churches.

During an event with people from the Diocese of Rome, Pope Francis addressed what he views as a perversion of spirituality: "Today too, there can be a rigid way of looking at things, one that restricts God's *makrothymía* (Greek for *long-suffering*), his patient, profound, broad and farsighted way of seeing things. God sees into the distance; God is not in a hurry. Rigidity is another perversion, a sin against the patience of God, a sin against God's sovereignty" (Francis 2021).

Many Catholics have told me that they wish LGBT Catholics would reform or to do penance before they can be considered full members of the Catholic Church. Likewise, several gay Catholics have told me they are doing penance every day to make up for their being gay.

Of course, this is not grounded in any solid theological understanding of the Catholic Faith. Yes, penance is an essential lesson in the *school of Jesus*, just as we learn more about the character of God every time we encounter someone through service. But the proper role of penance is not to make up for an error in God's creation, nor is it to be productive or to earn points. We must look up, gazing at

God the Father in awe, and allow ourselves to be transformed by that love rather than trying to discipline our way to holiness.

Jesus likens the discipline-first approach in difficult pastoral situations to a mob (John 8:3–11). He says the religious leaders should be aware of how difficult their rules are sometimes, especially when they do not create an environment that makes it easier on the people (Matt 23:4). And Jesus offers himself as the remedy to the mental exhaustion caused by the religious leader's overbearing rules when he says, "Come to me, all you that are weary and are carrying heavy burdens, and I will give you rest" (Matt 11:28). None of this discounts the importance of discipline, but instead warns us to spend a little bit more time on the discernment of God's will.

You also need to understand that whatever pain you are experiencing that makes you question your worth, there is also a heavenly father who desires to see you. And know that your suffering somehow imitates what Jesus experienced on the cross. Finally, our mother, Mary, warmly embraces you as her child.

See yourself and others just as God does. It will take some work and practice, but these are the tools of authentic spirituality.

"Thisness" and Discerning What Is Real

For years, I have attempted to understand specifically what some people mean when they say Catholic doctrine cannot change. If someone says doctrine is virtually unchangeable, then that is a much clearer statement. But rest assured, there are tons of examples of the Church learning more over the centuries about God's vastness and plan for his people. Ask the Vatican!

You don't need to dig that deep into the history books to see how our expression of doctrine has changed immensely over the centuries. It is constantly developing to more beautifully express the reality of God, who works with us to deepen our conscience and prepare us as a people to see his wonders.

Augustine and Aquinas were very clear that they wanted the Church to continue discovering. Otherwise it would mean we have turned off our brains to God's self-revelation to the human race. Both men recognized that our vocabulary and observations of the world lead us to new discoveries.

Doctrine is not a campaign. It is not a popular vote subject to our whims. God himself is immutable and expresses himself in the same way always. Yet he allows our consciences to deepen over time and to discover him in deeper and more beautiful ways.

If you would like to know more on this from major thought leaders of Catholic theology, I suggest googling "L'evoluzione della dottrina spiegata da Civiltà Cattolica" (The evolution of doctrine explained), which comes from an Italian website picking the brains of theologians working with the Vatican (Tornielli 2016). It is well worth taking a few minutes to read it using a web translator.

But the reason this causes so much difficulty for many Catholics is that they go to Confession, where they receive very unfortunate and bad advice.

First, it's important that the majority of priests are enthusiastic about imparting the mercy of God to others. But occasionally, even the best-intentioned priests can give advice that is not as relevant as they intended, or maybe it is even harmful. This is not a Catholic problem; this is just human nature.

A priest had encouraged me to hide my sexuality from others, including from other priests. I want to assume he meant well. He thought that by putting a lid on this element of my identity that it would keep me safe from harm. As mentioned above, unfortunately, that was not in my best interests, although it took me many years to unpack that.

Imagine that you have had a stomachache for months, and you start to be concerned that something is wrong. You start googling the best doctor to visit. It could be stress, your diet, or a more serious condition. On the doctor's office scheduling portal, you see that a specialist is available nearby, but the online reviews only show 1 out of 5 stars. Out of curiosity, you read the complaints in the reviews. Most patients said the doctor was busy and wrote prescriptions almost immediately before leaving for the next appointment. Some reviews say the treatment worked, but others had to return for a follow-up visit. The most common complaint may be that the doctor left questions about the patient's situation unanswered.

Although this doctor is probably very intelligent and has healed many people, the doctor is not entirely credible. Credibility would speak to how the patient assesses the expertise and reliability of the doctor concerning the experience or suffering of the patient.

Theology is not dissimilar, except it offers a path to holiness instead of offering health. Both fields of study pursue truth, desire to help others and require compassion.

Of course, anyone in the service industry should try to remember that people are not a statistic or an agenda, but a person created in the image of God. Consider the famous reminder from Jeremiah (1:5) that says, "Before I formed you in the womb I knew you, and before you were born, I consecrated you; I appointed you a prophet to the nations." You are not a mistake. Each one of us is a natural variant of God's creation, designed to reflect his brilliance and great depth.

And so theologians, confessors, psychologists, and anyone working to understand themself needs to have a balanced understanding of the "thisness" (this-ness) of the person seeking help, and how that relates to our place within creation. Thirteenth-century Franciscan theologian John Duns Scotus pioneered this subject within the study of philosophy.

Although he was eclipsed by the greatness of the philosophical works of St. Thomas Aquinas, Duns Scotus's model was just flexible and innovative enough for its time that he paved the way for the doctrine of the immaculate conception when others thought it was impossible. Scotus provides a new way of appreciating our place in God's creation, and to consider your uniqueness in the story of God's creation.

According to Blessed Duns Scotus, there is no one else that exists or ever will have existed that carries the same exact combination of physical traits, personal experiences, and memories as you. You do not have dignity and value based on your creation as male or female, but because specifically *you were intended by God* (Horan 2019, 151). Your uniqueness is a testament to God's creativity.

Thisness is not relativism. You cannot choose your natural eye color, hair color, brain structure, or the balance of hormones you are exposed to in the womb. You cannot preselect the organs you end up being born with from a menu, and you definitely cannot choose your sexual orientation. But, thanks to the development in our understanding of how complex the human person is, these facts can be agreed upon without any political or ideological agenda interfering.

We are, however, free to choose to love or be compassionate in a way that allows us to understand the broad scope of our complementarity to one another. Pursuing the truth means we might have to abandon old assumptions that neatly explain the world in black and white and instead surround ourselves with the diversity that allows us to understand the immense complexity and complementarity God beautifully designed and intended for us.

And so, returning to the analogy of the visit to the doctor's office, a doctor with five-star reviews is more likely to sit down with the patient and understand the wholeness of the person. Although the last twenty patients in a row may have been predictably suffering from simple heartburn, the doctor with five-star reviews listens to the patient, understands that more questions must be asked, and then performs some tests. *Aha!* This is actually a food allergy. A credible doctor does not assume that a typical patient always fits the textbook example. Everybody is a little bit different.

As we look at authentic spirituality, the question is not about a textbook response, but looking to the particular reality and trying to understand how best to order the particular case. In fact, Aquinas seemed to understand very well that we can use our gifts of reason to understand reality but that it is not a rigid set of rules but general principles (Aquinas n.d.). Just like reality, natural law is a flexible framework that is brilliantly capable of adapting to a wide range of circumstances.

St. Augustine felt this way too. Creation is not unchangeable. Its perfection can only be found through maturity and development. Catholic social teaching offers the world perhaps the best vision and principles of a society grounded in justice, but is less expert in offering ways to achieve it (Hawksley 2020, 112). There is a gap between our theoretical outlook and reality. Essentially, we still have a lot of sorting out to do to make sure the words we use in theology, the way we communicate them, and how they relate to the situations people face in real life. Bad theology begins with the idea already set, whereas good theology begins with reality.

This is why Pope Francis is asking Catholics to grow in their ability to discern. Commenting on the fact that many seminarians graduate, get ordained, and are thrown into difficult pastoral situations unprepared because the formation may have led them to counsel people from a rigidly defined a priori knowledge (from theoretical dedication instead of experience) (Spadaro 2018).

Authentic discernment also requires accompanying people in their suffering and their joy. A good theologian will have the ability to apply wisdom to concrete situations, which is why it is paramount that our bishops have more than just training in canon law. Speaking to Jesuits about authentic formation programs, "We need to truly understand this: in life not all is black on white or white on black… the shades of gray prevail in life" (McElwee 2016).

Going back to the original story, imagine if the doctor spent a full day with you, getting to know you and logging your symptoms. At the end of that day, when the doctor prescribes your medicine, you are likely to feel confident in their expertise and what they have prescribed.

In the same way, if a priest can build trust and get to know your experiences, you will be more likely to get good advice for your particular situation and the advice he has to share about the faith in general.

Chapter Four

RETHINKING CLARITY

THERE IS A DANGER in thinking that we have everything figured out. That does not mean we as Christians are in the wrong about our beliefs. Sacred tradition and scripture give us a great deal of confidence in the authority of the Church to speak about what is real or false. But resting in the collective knowledge that we already possess will surely stunt our spiritual growth.

No one should pretend to know all the unexpected twists and turns that theology could take, but it is safe to say the Church will continue to teach the essence of what it has always taught. And at the same time, our Church is very practical and tries to meet the very diverse needs of a flock that is growing in some countries while shrinking in others.

Sometimes, for practical reasons when teaching theology, we sacrifice depth. If you ask a priest how to become holy, there are a few different types of answers you might receive. One such way might sound more like a list: go to Mass, honor the commandments, confess your sins, follow the precepts of the Church, be good to your neighbors, obey the civil authorities. The list could go on for a while. You think to yourself: Check. Done. Ok. Will do But there is still something that seems to be lacking.

A second way of answering your question might be a much bolder but simpler command: "Become everything that God has willed for you as part of his creation."

The second is more credible as it is terrifying because in its simplicity, it still leaves you with a lifelong assignment of unpacking the world around you and learning how to seek God in new and more profound ways. It speaks to an authentic mission statement and urges the Christian to consider their gifts in connection to the universal Church.

However, the problem with that answer is that it's remarkably difficult to teach an entire world full of people what meaning and purpose really looks like! The early medieval Church feared giving people that broad assignment to learn on their own, and turned its full attention to human misdeeds, as explained in Fr. Jim Keenan's book *A History of Catholic Theological Ethics*, "Subsequently, sin is no longer our failure to bother to love, but rather a sspecific, vicious act....Even the works of mercy get caught into the obsession of sin" (Keenan 2022, 50).

Slowly, like a hammer staring down a nail, our Church began to see sin everywhere. The work of teaching priests to identify sins eventually turned toward actual printed handbooks that, from the eighteenth to twentieth centuries, held a completely negative opinion of sexual desires (Keenan 2022, 91). Can something that causes sin also be a gift? Not under such a clouded lens. In that context, it makes sense why so many have attempted to take sexuality and pathologize it, like a surgeon trying to remove a tumor. Did we put the same effort into recognizing and building up virtue?

Why did we create these lengthy manuals? Is it based in good theology? One of the greatest theologians the world has ever known, St. Thomas Aquinas, never thought it was possible to perfectly summarize the wide range of human behavior and distinctions in law. Thankfully the approach of using handbooks to identify sins has faded away in recent decades. We're going back to basics.

There is immense fear of helping people form their own consciences. Invoking one's conscience can be a tempting cop-out because it's hard for the outsider to judge your authenticity. Our role as Christians is to help people become the best disciples of Jesus Christ they are capable of realizing within their own lives. It is not a low standard. On the contrary, it is a high standard that requires a two-way openness to growth (in chapter 2 we discussed the story of the pagan Corneilius helping the apostle Peter reach a deeper conversion in Christ, too). Pope Francis has said that authentic theological work can't happen when we construct walls around it.

Throughout Christianity, the great theologians have had a general sense that they were deepening our understanding of the faith, setting it up so the next generation could discover even further. Many think that the phenomenal writings of St. Thomas Aquinas meant that theology had reached a peak and became sort of frozen for the remainder of human history. There is no evidence that Aquinas thought this. But I wonder if St. Thomas Aquinas and his brilliance has made us a little shy. Have we accepted all his conclusions about theology but are too timid to continue passing on his methods of discovery?

British cardinal-theologian St. John Henry Newman saw the unfolding theology as one of the exciting ideas about the Christianity. Authentic theology is not like origami unfolding in your brain, but instead it becomes recognizable through its applications in social life (Merrigan 2009).

It is not recognizable only in real life, but also through the shared testimony of Catholics talking about the importance of the sacraments in tackling vice and building up virtue in their lives. Listening and sharing testimony is one way we can test out our ideas about God.

Dr. Fabrizio Mastrofini, who has served at the Pontifical Academy for Life (an organization that works to build up the pope's defense for life), wrote an article on how theologians have always debated in the Church. It is often contentious, and sometimes when you compare what popes have said in different centuries it feels like they are contradicting each other. He said we shouldn't think of popes as going against one another, and instead wherever it seems there are "discontinuities" (breaks, or not a straight line) between popes, it is really in "fundamental continuity" with the Gospel (Mastrofini 2022).

Theology is always real and concrete. It is not meant to be abstract. And when it is most authentic itself, it opens us up to love. If you think of the twelve apostles as our Church's first theologians, this is the mission Jesus left to them the night before he died, "By this everyone will know that you are my disciples, if you have love for one another" (John 13:35). The unchanging and unmovable task assigned to our theologians—under the guidance of the pope—is to continue building up the Christian people so that they unfold that love in a complex and ever-changing world.

Social Pact or Encounter?

The more polarized our society becomes, the more important it is that everyday Catholic can sort out what belongs to our common faith vs. what belongs to a specific social group of Catholics. It's not easy to do. They are not mutually exclusive. If you walk around parish parking lots, it is rare that you see an even 50/50 divide of political bumper stickers. When there are options, we gravitate to parishes of people who are just like us.

Both our faith and our faith community touch on deep questions about the gifts God has given us. But in a Church that claims to be truly universal, we believe that humans were made to live our faith in communities of different kinds, meant to give gifts that help the community fulfill what it is otherwise lacking without your participation, and for us to discover the deepness of God encountering our differences within the sacraments. It requires an immense amount of effort to reject selfishness.

When someone says they are spiritual but not religious, I think they are attempting to divorce themselves from a "social pact." There is not an insignificant number of people who have been entirely unable to find a parish that is interested in what they have to offer, or unwilling to welcome someone so different than the rest of the attendees. An article in the *National Catholic Reporter* highlighted the work of Dr. Lawrence Cunningham, who described one of the roles of faith communities as to "provide refuge from the pressures and fears (real or imagined) of social change and/or disruption. The close bonds of such groups set up a kind of umbrella under which people can feel secure" (Manson 2011).

But the security and refuge that we demand from our parishes has consequences. By shutting out the world, we are also shutting out the fullness of reality. From that point, it becomes too easy to fall victim to error by thinking we have consulted everyone, when really we have just asked those exactly like us.

In the thirteenth century, Catholic theology contemplated that nature made women and disabled people without authority (Grillo 2020). The argument of that day and age was to assume that if God wanted to endow authority on a particular soul, they would have been born a man of stature. Does that idea reflect our current understanding of human dignity? Is nature and God's design the reason women were incapable of having any sort of authority, or was it a social pact that we had created for ourselves? Under the theology of the thirteenth century, it would have been entirely impossible for Franklin Delano Roosevelt to authentically have served as president of the United States. Yet, he served the most terms of any president in American history. Was his authority made up? Or had our theology of the past reflected a social pact? Did our past have an incomplete understanding of nature?

Although this book will later contemplate the relationship between developing authentic theology, sacred tradition, and listening to testimony, we will first turn to thinking about your own creation in the image and likeness of God.

Creation in God's Image

Knowing how to apply theology and making it concrete in your life starts with knowing who you are. For example, you might think of yourself as a traditional Catholic, an American, and a conservative. Those are three external identities that explain how someone interacts with the world. And those identities also inform each other, even if the person doesn't prioritize 100 percent of each value sets equally at all times.

However, this book is less concerned with social pacts and external identities, and instead seeks to prepare you to identify the essential realities that God gave you. What are the things about you that could not possibly change because you would no longer be wholly *you*?

Maybe you knew a young athlete who thinks of themself as a really good "soccer player" but later in life becomes too old or injured to play. Instead of changing their identity to "former soccer player," they now start to draw on the core identities that speak to their character: a leader, a team player, and so on.

Actually, the lifelong process of understanding our intrinsic identities as created by God gives a great deal of purpose and excitement to the meaning of life. One of St. John Paul II's cardinals, Avery Dulles, said, "This life, flowing outwards, pulsates through many subjects, draws them together, and brings them into union with their source and goal" (Horan 2019, 5). Now we're starting to get a little bit closer to understanding the internal identities that make us who we are.

The idea of catholicity is that we're moving toward the wholeness of reality. That's the purpose of theology. The completeness we are aiming for in understanding our creation in the image and likeness of God is a lifelong process that requires authenticity, prayer, and community if we want to understand it—at least in the Christian sense.

It is quite common for some priests in very traditional parishes to reach out to me and respectfully ask me not to say being "gay" is one of those essential characteristics that God gave me. But it is! The Vatican even declared half a century ago, "The human person is so profoundly affected by sexuality that it must be considered as one of the factors which give to each individual's life the principal traits that distinguish it" (Sacred Congregation for Doctrine of the Faith, 1975). It's far from being the only big part of my identity, but it is a trait that helps to explain how I relate to others, and how I see the world. That is part of the gift of individuality that God gave to me. My duty is to learn how my traits lend an effort to give honor to God, my community, and family.

But what if I accepted that invitation to pathologize or sanitize one of my traits? Would that be consistent with *wholeness*? No! The theology in book tries to underscore that we have to learn to love the life that God gifted to us. And I refuse to allow unbridled honesty to ever be a reason why I'd have to give up being a part of traditional Catholic circles. Neither should you. At the end of the day, even though there are disagreements on the discipline, the crux and core of my theology is the same.

To me, being Catholic means loving how God made us, including the many peculiarities that come with that, and learning how to overcome the biases that other people have taught us.

That is what my personal experiences have been like as an American LGBT Catholic. I feel both well-represented and sometimes like my identities are in conflict. Some days it feels like everything is in sync. I never want to hear the various sides bashing one another, yet that is often what happens.

Even though your experiences will be unique and specific to you, it is important to realize that each of your identities are real. And Jesus has no problem trying to come closer to you within each of the identities you are living.

In the Bible, Jesus repeatedly works to reach across the various identities: Jews, Samaritans, and Gentiles. Remember that all these reference points take place within a geographic area about the size of Delaware. These were the great culture wars of the first century.

Yet despite a rather lengthy list of the things the Jews and Samaritans have in common, their cultures decide to focus on the differences. Does this make sense? Is this division really of God's own design or from ourselves?

LGBT and other unwanted Catholics often get caught up in the culture wars taking place all around them. It mimics some of the divisions we see in the Bible. As noted earlier, in many parts of the world (and especially in English-speaking countries), the attitudes toward Catholics are becoming increasingly more biased. So it is fair, if you find yourself in Confession and it seems the priest is being unfair or asking something unholy of you, just remind him politely, "Father, I am here for mercy." If you are comfortable and firmly understand who you are as a created child of God, invite him to pray with you at a later time and ask to talk about this in further detail.

Especially if you have an encounter in the sacrament of Confession that feels like you are being judged harshly, just for the sake of understanding where the priest is likely coming from it's worth thinking about the role of the father as a figurehead of the community. The way we think of the Ten Commandments has changed quite a bit since the early days. If you ask someone who has lived on a college campus, the many rules they agreed to as part of "residence life" were very similar to the way the ancient Hebrews thought of the Ten Commandments. They were rules for maintaining a healthy and bonded community.

We can go one step further because although a college may "love" its students, it isn't anywhere near the extreme and radical depths of the God's love for his chosen people. These ground rules known as the Ten Commandments were proof that God wanted to ensure a lasting community.

When you fast forward to the life of Jesus, as moral theologian Professor Mauro Bianchi says, the Gospel attempts to portray moral theology in a much simpler way. This makes it more convincing to the larger audience. It can be labeled a simpler way because it does not encourage the listener to build a relationship with the historical Jesus who lived two thousand years ago, but with the Jesus who eternally lives thanks to his resurrection at Easter (Bianchi 2014). Of course, Catholics do not discard the importance or continued relevance of the Ten Commandments, but our focus is less on perpetuating a community from thousands of years ago, and instead on building a relationship with Christ for the life to come. Just as the Jewish people were given a set of rules relevant to their situation, what are the particular ways that you are being called to live a life of virtue in pursuit of Jesus Christ?

We believe the resurrection of Jesus Christ means something real for every identity, every community, at every place and time. Reflecting on the identities you carry, the next time you go to Mass and receive the Eucharist, do so with an open mind and a prayerful plea to ask the Lord to transform you to be more like him. In this Eucharistic encounter, may you learn to love yourself just as God does.

Walk with confidence knowing that while you search for Jesus Christ in the Eucharist, he also searches for you too. Like he did for the woman at the well, Jesus would walk through a desert in hostile territory just to ask you for your gift, your presence, and to enjoy a cup of refreshing water with you (John 4:1–42). Above all, your creation as an individual is given to you in the likeness and image of God. Your creation as an individual, with all your uniqueness and peculiarities, is not a mistake.

The Scapegoat

Identities also carry risk. Whatever it is that you say you belong to, it always seems to create envy for others. The greater the envy, the deeper a line people tend to draw in the sand.

Think back to your first day at a new school. Think back to a time when suddenly you were in a large room where nobody knew one another. Even think of being assigned to jury duty and realizing you are about to spend eight hours a day with other jurors you know nothing about. How do you start building a connection?

The easy answer: find something that everyone loves to hate.

Is it true? The easiest way to build trust in a group is to find someone everyone hates?

French philosopher René Girard wondered about that too. Why would the Samaritans and Jews, two opposing camps that are more culturally similar than they are dissimilar, decide to draw borders, live on their land alone, and proclaim that holiness and truth belong to them? Why are ethnicities trapped within borders drawn by humans? Was it divine revelation? Perhaps. But Jesus Christ himself was not a neutral party. Jesus was a faithful and devout Jew. Yet, at the same time, he dared to walk through Samaria and made an unwanted Samaritan woman his first missionary to the Gentiles.

In his theory on *mimetic desire*, Girard says that human nature draws us to try and imitate or desire what we do not have. Humans are almost innately aware that we are made for something more significant, so we start to look to other humans to teach us how to be who we are. This leads to rivalries and groups drawing distinctions about one another, eventually manifesting in violence (Lefebure 1996). It's like a perversion of the theology of the "image of God," that we are created in God's likeness.

This happens within politics too. Consider your opinion of whether there is a great deal of difference between Republicans and Democrats. In 2022, polling found that most Americans think the other party is immoral, closed-minded, and dishonest (Pew Research Center 2022). It always seems to be the *other* party. The divisive power split means both sides fight as hard as they can for the same limited pool of resources to help their respective people. *We cannot have peace until our side is victorious!* The reality is that parties in the United States were seen only a decade ago as ideologically moderate, or at least managed by centrists (Ball 2014). Yet the apocalyptic language about the others would suggest we are in a battle for heaven and earth.

The idea that the two political parties are not actually conservative or liberal enough gets at the heart of what Girard says about mimetics. We develop a purity test because it will preserve our values. It becomes the burden of group leaders to rid the community of those with diverse opinions challenging the group dynamics. And sooner rather than later, we conclude that our lives would be so much better if this one person would just go away. This is what Girard calls a scapegoat.

Scapegoats can take many forms. But the basic premise is that a group of people place their woes on an individual or a defenseless minority group and then push them out of the fold.

Girard thinks that Jesus Christ is the ultimate example within the Bible of a scapegoat. Jesus' message of inclusion and salvation for all—not just those the leaders of the day who were considered worthy—was met with violence. When a rebellion was brewing and both the Romans and Jews feared what would happen next, they offered the political prisoner Jesus as a "ritual sacrifice (crucifixion) to achieve a specific outcome (increased unity and peace)" (Burgis 2021). Jesus became the victim when he was sacrificed on the cross.

However, the brilliance of the story is found in the Resurrection. God himself found favor with the victim and not the oppressor. God responded to persecution and violence with the opposite values (Lefebure 1996). And for the first time in history, the victim (Jesus Christ) who was pushed outside the boundaries of the community came back!

And through the death of the victim and his resurrection, the boundaries set by the religious leaders were utterly shattered. Salvation is now accessible to all.

Different groups will inevitably take turns being the scapegoat. It's just how human nature works. But we are not called to sit idly by. Catholics are called to be prophetic, and to stand up and declare themselves as made in the image of God, and that Jesus Christ himself made this tactic null and void in a sense of Church ethics.

Echoing the vision Peter received from an angel when he was shockingly told to go visit a group of pagans, "What God has made clean, you are not to call profane. What God has made clean, you are not to call profane. What God has made clean, you are not to call profane."

You, too, have been made clean.

Being Gay

Remember the theory of mimetics from the last section as you think more about who you actually are, not who other people say you are supposed to be. As quoted in the book *Wanting*, René Girard said, "I think the reason we talk so much about sex is that we don't dare talk about envy" (Burgis 2021, 158). When people realize you are different, possess unique talents, have access to culture in a way they do not, and so on, if they cannot find a way to realize those same things in their life it leads to a desire to impose control on you. Envy becomes a sin that reinvents itself as righteousness.

It seems impossible, but the lifelong challenge of overcoming these mimetic desires is only successful when met with authenticity. These are things you will need to sort out for yourself.

There are seemingly opposing pressures in the world facing every young adult these days. The first is an ultra-modern pressure that says *individualism before everything else*. That attitude is a complicated rejection of God's commandments, which were given to us as a sort of *community rules* because he wants us to thrive together.

But at the same time that it opposes God's ideals for community life, in some ways it more successfully grasps the theological concept that you are unique. God has not, nor will he ever repeat the exact combination of traits and qualities that make you unique. Your individuality reflects his vast creativeness that is beyond all human comprehension.

The second worldly pressure is an extreme religious discipline that holds *conformity before everything else*. Yes, I am respectfully calling a specific kind of religious discipline a worldly pressure because just like individualism it is complicated in how successfully it grasps some theological concepts while deprioritizing others. Conformity can help keep a religious family together during tough times, but it does not necessarily lead to holiness. Holiness is not about staying within boundaries, but about orienting your life upward and becoming all that God meant for you. As far as sexuality goes, there are conformist attitudes within many Christian communities that regrettably reduce and impoverish the experience of love to nothing more than a structural exchange (or exchange of body parts).

Our philosophers of long ago understood sex and sexuality in ways that made sense for the observations of their day but that were scientifically incorrect. Getting us back on track to a proper anthropological standard will take time. For example, the female form was understood to be lesser in value because she simply receives the seed of life from a man during sex (Horan 2019). They did not know that both the male and female forms have something critical to offer (sperm and egg). How could they have known? They couldn't have. The ancient philosophers based their belief on the best form of science available at the time: observation. In a sense, you could say the invention of a microscope impacted the trajectory of theology in positive way because it started us off on this path of opening our hearts and recognizing gifts that exist within our differences.

Do not ever rush to change or challenge the teachings of the Church! Yes, it is a fair critique that we had overstructuralized our ideas on sex, at times reducing it a simple donation by a man, and that we continue to deemphasize that couples relate to each other in different ways. But authenticity takes time, and it is important that we walk together as a Church. Dr. Mastrofini points out that even the encyclical (a document written by the pope meant to teach) on married love and human life (*Humanae Vitae*) falls within reformable doctrine. But even though is reformable, it was issued by the pope in his authority and should be respected as such (Mastrofini 2022). Often, theologians work to help the Church balance out their teachings the same way a nutritionist may point out the things missing from your plate.

This book is not campaigning for a change in teaching. This book is urging the reader to begin by looking inside yourself. Understand your own gifts and the responsibilities that come from that. Archbishop Delpini of Milan sent guidance to all the parishes in his area on topic of sexuality with, "Being a man, being a woman is a gift. I am this man, I am this woman. The body, in all its aspects… is not a prison that mortifies the person, but the condition for establishing loving relationships in the form of reciprocity." He went on to say that every Christian should welcome their own individual traits as a context for their own calling in life (Delpini 2023).

None of us is created to live in a prison, no matter how badly we want to judge ourselves harshly on our health, abilities or disabilities, or sexuality. This is no less true for those who are gay. As we try out the theology for ourselves, it's healthy to consider all the parts that make up our unique and God-given identities, the things about us that are immutable (unchanging).

Tomorrow, as you walk down a busy street or sit in traffic, take notice of every stranger you pass and imagine they are holding a nicely wrapped Christmas present. Each gift is free, unique, speaks to who they are, and can help us better understand ourselves. Make an extra effort to see these gifts in the hands of the homeless, the people we ignore as we look for a seat on the bus, and people from the LGBT community.

That is how God sees you. He sees the gifts he provided you with. And God is excited for you to develop these in communion with others and his creation. And we are called to take our talents, our intelligence, and whatever gifts we were given through our unique participation in the human mystery, and lovingly decide to offer them justly, freely, and lovingly to others (Lawler and Salzman 2022).

One of the most influential theologians of the twentieth century, Karl Rahner, believed God revealed the deepest mysteries about himself in becoming human. Jesus Christ was not pretending to be human, but he actually became human (O'Brien 2004).

And in assuming all human nature, he has given the human experience a new and complete meaning. This is an assurance of your dignity exactly as you are.

Once you know who you are, and are assured of God's love for you, it becomes possible to take all your traits and structure them in virtue.

More and more, the theologians, the bishops, and now the popes see sexuality as a gift, and less of a hindrance to holiness. That is why the archbishop of Milan referred to sexuality as the "experience of love and the different nuances of attraction" (Delpini 2023). It is real!

And so the Church does not have the ability to determine your sexual orientation on your behalf any more than you do. The fact that we now know sexuality isn't chosen presents a major challenge to the old legalistic way of understanding the human person.

Sacramental theologian Dr. Andrea Grillo presents a more mature Catholic approach that urges the faithful not to be bitter, but to allow faith to open the mind to God's greatest realities, and without limiting the surprises of the Holy Spirit. (Grillo 2022, 208).

In other words, he says each of us has a lifelong journey of trying to live as God created us. If we start with prefabricated answers about our sexuality, without any serious prayerful discernment of our creation, then we have not made an act of faith. And this is a common concern raised by moral theologians. We have separated our ethics and morals in the area of human sexuality from virtues. This is especially important in the field of natural law where the inclinations are important, and not just our actions themselves. We need to become more open-minded to orient our lives and sexuality to faith, hope, and charity.

Although this book dives into some of the more painful memories of Church history, it does not seek to make the reader bitter. It seeks to inaugurate processes of discernment that awaken you to whatever God is calling you to in life.

You were created perfectly. The eternal being willed that you have a soul and that you exist, that it was done by love and in conjunction with a cooperative act of love by your parents.

The fact that so many LGBT youth consider suicide or feel the need to leave the Church means that we have not yet fully understood what it means to be created in God's image, that we are expressing it in the wrong way, or that the collective Church community is ignoring its responsibility to seek the full communion with God's creation we were designed for.

How do we understand the book of Genesis 1:27 when it says God created male and female? Well, if you are a lawyer, you might be satisfied knowing that there are two legally distinct entities in that story: man and woman. But theologians are more curious about what makes us different and why God didn't create just one single gender of human. Horan notes that the Bible is not describing two half-persons (man and woman), but instead, God shows us right from the beginning that he creates us with differences. We should be thankful that all humans are not designed to experience the world identically, for we each share equally in the fullness of human nature (Horan 2019).

Going further than that, our genetic traits—including those we would not have freely chosen for ourselves—and handicaps do not preclude that we were created in God's image and likeness. For we are all formed as "visible images of the invisible God" (Francis 2020). And in a very particular sense, every kind of suffering, including mental illness, resembles Christ's crucifixion and shares the likeness of Christ in a concrete way (Honings 1996).

It should not surprise you that Catholics are at the forefront of the movement to recognize the full dignity and rights of all people who experience disabilities. The norm for special education used to be enrolling children on a separate track and removing them from the regular classroom. However, school systems increasingly find that inclusive classrooms can offer a two-way-street benefit. In our willingness to encounter people on the margins, we often find they have something to teach us.

Five years into the Pope Francis papacy, a Catholic theologian from South Africa intentionally and provocatively posted a link online to the book *You Have to Be Gay to Know God* by Siyathokoza Khumalo. People were surprised. But, of course, the priest's point was straightforward: to fully understand Jesus Christ's experiences, you must have been rejected by your own religious congregation. Perhaps that simple, provocative post could also prompt the question: "If I am gay, am I also made in the image of God?" The answer is as equally affirmative for the LGBT or unwanted Catholic as it is for any other created person.

A Church That Is Learning Lessons

On a visit to an Iñupiat (indigenous people and culture) village in Alaska, an elder told me the story of how the state government set the hunting season for a time of year when the birds did not even migrate through their area of the state. The state capitol is more than one thousand miles away from this village so unless they make a special effort, the villagers and the state government hunting authorities don't have a lot of opportunity to encounter one another.

Even though it was outside of the Alaska-approved hunting season, the villagers went out and hunted when the birds finally arrived in their area. The government authorities learned about this and immediately sent up law enforcement to arrest the hunters. The elders of the village made sure to put a bird in the hand of every person in that town, saying, "Arrest us all!" According to the story that elder shared with us, it took a tense encounter for the state government to realize that the rules they issued weren't as relevant to everyone's situation as they thought.

Your Church, too, is learning how to become a more loving Church. In some countries, mainly where there is a more robust tradition of appointing bishops who have a terminal degree in canon law, it is less likely that theology in any area is going to develop and grow.

Typically, these bishops were selected for their important abilities to keep the family together during times of complex change. In other countries, particularly where terminal degrees in moral theology are the norm for bishops, you are very likely to see development.

It is important to remember that the law never constrains reality, and that our Church law naturally develops more slowly and more separately from whatever pace our understanding of the world changes. So not only do we have to avoid constraining theology with existing Church law, but we must avoid applying our own lenses.

Professor Andrea Grillo points out that an absolutist view can lead us to believe something is natural or not natural solely because it goes against the grain of what we are used to experiencing. In an article raising theological points about how to classify variants of sexuality under natural law, he points out that Aquinas's *Summa Theologica* argued that people with disabilities or those born to unmarried parents could not become Catholic priests (Grillo 2020). They were assumed to be defective. In those cases, the people were from a world not known by Aquinas. But let's not disparage St. Aquinas. No! In fact, he took ideas that were entirely stagnant and got the conversations moving forward again. When we look at his place in Christian history you can see how the Holy Spirit guided his sensational ability to write about reality in ways never thought of before.

And once again, something extraordinary happens when we open ourselves to the Holy Spirit. We realize that God created people with gifts we did not even think possible. Just think of Fr. Stu Long, portrayed by Mark Wahlberg in the 2022 movie *Father Stu*.

The real-life priest was primarily confined to ministry from a nursing home, which proved to be an inspiring and relatable story for so many. According to the common understanding of natural law in earlier centuries, inspiring stories like this were thought theologically impossible. We used to focus on the man's structural—or physical—integrity to try and understand God's will for him. Now, we also try to understand their intellectual and relational abilities.

> The horizon must be truly open. And to this openness there corresponds an "incomplete thinking," an "open thinking." Francis once asked, "Do I let myself be 'unhinged inside' by paradox?…God is creative; he is not closed, and that is why he is never rigid. God is not rigid!" (Spadaro 2023)

There are a few other moments in history where some representatives of the Church responded more harshly to *the outsider* than we would care to admit. Those stories often begin with what at first appears to be a heroic defense of truth. For example, a lower-class girl from France named Joan of Arc led an army to battle against the English.

She was fighting in the name of God!

Especially for such an unlikely heroine, she was doing so with quite a bit of conviction and popularity! The bishops of England were afraid she could tip the scales in France's favor, but also, how could she really be a representative of God if she were fighting against them? She was ultimately declared a heretic at the hands of the English bishops and put to death. Now that history and the universal Church have had centuries to review her legacy, she is recognized as a saint in the worldwide Catholic Church.

Of course, it's fair to gently point out that St. Joan of Arc's position is also difficult to reconcile. Although considering her background and the way she handled herself, her story is not intended to highlight her reputation as a political revolutionary or even a theologian.

On the contrary, at least in the way the story has been handed down, Joan was a humble girl who did brave and courageous tasks for the sole reason that she discerned God had called her to it. And when that meant facing death, she refused to be disobedient to what God had called her to do. She is a prototype example of the *primacy of conscience* in practice.

Returning to the primary concern, the fact that Catholic bishops of one country occasionally pitted their own interpretations against one other contributed to the reasons that the universal Church needed the maturity of Vatican II. We are no longer a community where one bishop speaks about the God who chooses England while others speak of the God of Germany. Created in the image of God, we are all designed to be in communion, so the way we live our faith should reflect that.

This also happened to some extent during World War I, where scholars observed that Christian leaders, including some Catholic bishops, became wrapped up in the energy of patriotism (Reeves 2015) and that some Catholic leaders across Europe began to paint the "other" as the enemy. Several prominent Catholic bishops in Austria told the faithful that the foreign attacks on the ruling family was cause for a "just war" because it was in defense of legitimate authority, and because of this Catholics began to see their national loyalty as sign of their commitment to faith (Houlihan 2015, 52). That enthusiasm can sweep congregations off their feet at first and maybe even grow the congregation for a decade or so.

But following the destruction and hell on earth that so many in Europe experienced, it started to become increasingly more difficult to explain whether we still thought God was on our side.

As has been said already, theology is simply an attempt for finite humans to use their vocabulary to describe an infinite reality. It doesn't have an agenda or a side. And at the same time, an authentic theology deeply reflects a sense of justice. This lesson reflects why theology must be exceptionally careful not to be influenced by political parties, whose leaders will eventually come and go with time and as the national interest changes.

Weeks after the start of World War II, the still very new pope, Pius XII, did his best to take on the swelling anger taking shape around the globe. Invoking his status as the universal shepherd of Catholics everywhere, he issued an urgent document called *Summi Pontificatus* (Of the Supreme Pope) on the topics of unity in humanity (1939). We have to be clear-eyed; the problem was not simply on the German side. In fact, many German bishops worked exceptionally hard to promote peace, reject extreme nationalism, and at the same time, protect Catholics from persecution. Yet the appeal for unity was too late and fell on deaf ears.

Consider what it would have been like on the eve of World War II in 1939. Imagine knowing that you might be drafted to fight if things get bad. You may have only been a few years old when the previous global conflict ended. The previous two decades brought about an economic boom and bust, women voting in elections, and the rebuilding of town squares. At the same time, the utter destruction of human life and property that your family witnessed has left you wondering if you still really believe in God.

As you prepare for the possibility of war, you remember that the priest and the bishop still have an overall good reputation in the community, despite their congregations being smaller. As you wait to see if you will be drafted to fight, you listen to their words in case they have any wisdom to share. In that situation, if you were sitting in the congregation of a bishop who rallied you to fight for the patriotic cause, you would have felt inspired to fight. Because God is on your side.

Just as it was in the earlier First World War, many of our clergy seized on the strong emotions running through their countries as opportunity to bolster church attendance and interest in the faith (Houlihan 2015, 112). On one hand, we should always have a robust energy for sharing the faith in times of crisis, but never to the extent that it encourages continued disunity across humanity. As St. Bruno said about the cross standing firm while the world turns, there will always be a temptation to use Jesus to bolster our claims to superiority. But the cross is a call to universal love and therefore has no interest in deeming one side superior.

The unimaginable pains of the holocaust, the nuclear bombs, and the continent flattened by fighting put an end to this idea once and for all—at least in many parts of Europe. When we try to apply the idea of God to our own interests, it results in *ideology* instead of theology.

The point of this book is not to argue whether any war is just or unjust, nor is it a lack of full appreciation for the sacrifices of millions to end the two World Wars. This book does point out that there were a certain number of bishops on both sides claiming God was on their side. And yet the humanity of Europe was nearly destroyed, and it is somewhat astonishing that it has recovered. These existential issues should drive theological discernment and development.

We can apply the wisdom of Catholic Europe to the crises the Church is facing in the modern world. Without falling into theological error, our leaders have sometimes pushed hard against what are viewed as competing or emerging political and cultural powers. We must be vigilant not to let our leaders trample on the rights of freedom of religion. These are tricky things to balance.

Yet ideological lenses continue in certain parts of the Church, particularly where poverty isn't quite as systemic, and the people do not know what it is like to have a war on their land. Human desire is naturally to hold onto a familiar and static understanding of the world and assume that whatever is new must be wrong. This is a coping mechanism, and understandably so because many people desire their church to be a safe haven from modernity.

But in the modern world, recognizing the theology of "God is on our side," is rarely as obvious as hearing someone say that phrase outright. As we learned above, any time an institution faces a decline or is losing members of other forms of power to the outside world, it creates hard feelings. Revisiting the point made at the beginning of this book, when religious people enforce boundaries, it is not necessarily evidence that they are bad people. They have a tough job in modern society, and LGBT youths who are struggling may have tried working with one of the few clerics who prioritizes discipline first. It is usually intended in a loving way, in hopes of not disrupting the togetherness of the Catholic family. But if you experienced that, you deserve better.

This can be applied to the narrative against LGBT and divorced persons, who often feel as if they are relegated to second-class citizens in the Church. It sometimes takes on a life of its own to the point that we, as Catholics, start to see ourselves as the victim. Some priests warn that good Catholics keep their distance from those who do not share the same values. This book has already explored why that technique is not a mature approach to faith but instead is akin to how one would set boundaries for a child who only understands the word *no*. There is no basis for this behavior within an authentic catholicity. The priority should always be highlighting each individual's design in God's image, regardless of their traits and life experiences.

Cardinal Czerny of Canada has said that Vatican II intended to flip the narrative so that the Church now presents its ideas to the modern world in dialogue, ending the practice of acting as a "stronghold besieged by internal and external enemies" (Czerny 2022). The theological approach of Vatican II seems more confident, more trusting, and more open to reality. As was stated already, theology is not a "truth" that can be possessed, but simply an effort to use our finite human vocabulary to express an infinite divine reality.

The lessons we have learned in encountering people in different cultures can also be applied to LGBT Catholics. The Catholic Church believes that the authentic evangelization we perceive as outsiders not only shows us new ways to bring the faith to others, but also helps us to become better Christians.

For if we are all designed to be in communion, how can we consider our picture of reality and theology to be complete without them? Cardinal Czerny expressed the same lesson that Peter learned in meeting the pagan Cornelius (Acts 10): "The inculturation of faith is a two-way process: if the Church in delivering the Word of God offers the possibility for all cultures to discover a meaning and purpose to human existence, at the same time, by encountering visions of humanity that emerge from other cultures, she discovers how new facets of the mystery are revealed" (Czerny and Barone 2023).

Chapter Five

DEVELOPING FAITHFUL THEOLOGY

THIS SECTION EXPLORES how doctrine authentically develops, and the direction in which it may be going for LGBT and others who feel they are outsiders.

As recommended earlier, for any reader who would like to verify the following perspectives on doctrinal development for themselves, I recommend searching online for "L'evoluzione della dottrina spiegata da 'Civiltà Cattolica'" by Andrea Tornielli in *La Stampa* in 2016. This archive is a freely accessible version of La Civiltà Cattolica's perspective, a publication that is edited by the Vatican Secretariat of State.

The Earth Revolves Around the Sun: Now What?

Theologians have been speculating for decades about what it would mean for Christian anthropology if we ever learned that sexual orientation might be something other than a rebellious choice. Well, here we are.

Before getting to that point, it's worth imagining ourselves sitting in the background as Church officials debated Galileo Galilei's findings in 1613. He declared that science had proven the Earth revolves around the Sun. You are probably wondering what part of that is controversial. One would think this is a rather strange problem for theologians to worry about.

Why was it so threatening? Well, there are at least a few considerations. Consider how quickly the tide of Protestantism was spreading around parts of Europe. New ideas were scary because they could lead to more splits in the Church, so they had to be investigated.

Is it possible that the harsh reception Galileo received was more about the angst of a rapidly changing world? Probably. Aristotle was one of the first philosophers to identify that the Sun revolved around the Earth, and everyone accepted it. That's not a terrible assumption based on the scientific tools available three hundred years before the birth of Jesus. Aristotle was also the forerunner of natural law that St. Aquinas spent so much time developing.

So, if we were to allow someone to upend twenty centuries of human understanding, would it invite chaos into our faith in principles such as the natural law as well? It makes sense why some people may be afraid that science could overtake divine revelation or the authorities on faith and morals. But on the issue of heliocentrism, the Church eventually realized that we had to mature. That is because we do not hold onto an ideology as much as we try to reflect reality as God designed the world. What a beautiful thing, to realize that the Church is not threatened by authentic science.

A seminarian once told me that society now knows quite a bit more about human sexuality than it did decades ago, but he said that it more likely requires a pastoral change and not a modification of Church teaching. To be fair, I would never recommend that a seminarian challenge Church teaching—that is a time to absorb and discern a very important vocational calling in our world.

However, it struck me as interesting that someone could admit there is new information that challenges our assumptions about the world, but it's okay to ignore that, at least as far as proclaiming "truth" to the world.

The reality is that the Catholic Church stopped prosecuting people for teaching the heresy of "the Earth revolves around the Sun," long before it issued an official change in teaching. My best guess is that will happen on teachings of human sexuality as well. Unity is important, so it does matter that we allow people to reflect and learn in their own time.

But the Church does have the obligation to help people understand how to live their lives in accordance with their design, even when there is tension over the official teachings. The Catechism stresses the importance of forming strong Catholic consciences and following that judgment, even in the rare case where there is tension with Church teaching.

In the long run, we cannot simply excuse old assumptions to act as a justification for our beliefs. That is inconsistent with "truth." The Catholic Church is more than capable of adapting here too because it is alive and constantly deepening in conscience with the help of the Holy Spirit. These developments make future generations better Catholics.

HOW ABOUT HUMAN SEXUALITY?

Let's start with the very firm warning of St. Paul, who says we must guard the faith that was handed on to us (1 Tim 6:20–21). Moral theologians in the Church have been working to help the magisterium sort out the truths of divine revelation and natural law, while at the same time helping us put aside old cultural lenses and assumptions that distract us from the main idea. I don't envy them. Our theologians have a tough job.

There are some things that will always remain true. We give glory to God when we live in a way that honors how he designed us. A proper Catholic ethic on human sexuality will be rooted in the natural law. Essentially, we want to help people take their natural tendencies, desires, and dreams and help orient them so that they give glory to God.

Just as the Church had to recalibrate its teachings on whether the Sun revolves around the Earth, it has also had to correct course on the naturalness of slavery. If we think of theology as a beautiful plant that grows, does it also need to be pruned? In this case, our teachings on slavery appeared at a surface level to make sense, but they were blocking sunlight from promoting growth on the branch known as human dignity. Since then, theologians have been aware of the possibility that other issues need to be pruned. But they do so with exceptional care. It is a high bar. The issue of sexuality is one that Greek professor of moral theology, marriage, and ethics Fr. Basilio Petrà feels is next, "This passage is possible—I believe—without any contradiction. Just as we have passed without contradiction from the natural givenness of slavery to its unnaturalness, in the same way we can pass from the unnaturalness of homosexuality to its natural givenness without harming the moral normative nature of love in any way" (Petrà 2021, 126).

What gave him such a convincing reason to reconsider the teaching as it already exists? Those holding doctorates in moral theology are seemingly at consensus that, around 400 years ago, we started to reduce the importance of natural law in a meaningful way when it comes to sexual ethics.

Theologian James Keenan found that Church law and discipline governing human sexuality started to split from its own teachings. It became "pulled away from their integral relationship with inclinations and virtues and reduced to a set of principles and precepts without really any theological anthropology that considers who the human being is as created" (Keenan 2022, 217). We cannot talk about judging human desires without also trying to understand how they drive us toward virtue.

Doctor of Sacred Theology Cardinal Robert McElroy, made

the same observation about the split between theology and Church law in the seventeenth century, saying our teachings on human sexuality became "abstract, deductivist, and truncated," whereas he advocates a return to the much more complicated, messy, and drawn-out way of teaching the community about the path to holiness (McElroy 2023).

Theology is an expression of reality. And so, it should be capable of explaining in a beautiful way the entire human person and our design in God's plan. That does not mean the path to holiness is easy. Not at all. But a great deal of freedom is involved when we orient our whole selves in accordance with how we were made.

A GUT CHECK FOR PASTORAL MINISTRY

This section is a reflection on how my personal experiences being ministered to failed to teach me authenticity and how to stand up for myself. Pastoral ministry focuses on the spiritual needs of individuals, but before learning more about theology, I attempted to do this primarily by following rules and disciplines. Eventually that left me craving something more. The reality is social unrest, crises of unity, and debates about values have all helped shaped the development of doctrine. That is why understanding any current crises the Church is facing along with the spiritual needs of the people always links back to Church teaching.

The world is changing fast, yet our doctrine on sexuality continues to be taught from a perspective that focuses solely on the complementarity of body parts—something psychology has long moved on from in favor of an approach that looks at the whole person and their ability to relate to another (Lawler and Salzman 2022). Likewise on the topic of sin, Professor Keenan carefully but importantly points out that masturbation was held by the Church in previous centuries as more grave than rape (Keenan 2023). And so as you can imagine, we've already come a long way in balancing out the way we talk about things. But we still have far to go.

To people facing complex family situations, the credibility of our ministry largely rests on our willingness to understand difficult subjects in light of human dignity. For example, a homeless ministry based in a church basement once faced resistance from individuals who didn't like to sit next to them at Mass. Whether it was because the homeless were strangers or for other reasons, some people were uncomfortable. Several people floated the idea of adding restrictions to where the homeless can go on the property. Well of course, as soon as you tell someone you love them, but there are the strings attached (in this case asking some individuals not to fully participate in parish life), they immediately sense that the parish does not actually care for them. Maybe they'll still take the food you offer and say thank you with a smile, but the ministry will never have a breakthrough in reaching their hearts. The restrictionism cheats both the parish volunteer and the person seeking out help of the grace that comes from encountering one another.

Ministry should always be an opportunity to see the person we care for as an encounter with the risen Christ. Jesus himself wandered and preached. Imagine the grime that accumulated on his clothes. If we magically visited the first century and spotted him asking for water at the well, would he not resemble a beggar?

The restrictionism attitude can be found in a lot of places in ministry and for a lot of different groups of people. The overemphasis on talking about body parts has in a way cheated the incredible value of *chastity*. In school, you were probably taught that chastity is about not having sex (which is actually celibacy). What does that look like? We could examine a long list of rules, or we could try to apply the virtue to the whole of the relationship. *Chastity* always wants the best for the other, refuses to control the partner, and never possesses the partner (Francis 2024).

In ministering to couples and young adults, why would we ever restrict the idea of chastity to sexual acts? It can also be about rooting relationships in healthy, nontoxic practices. The virtue of chastity is another function born out of the command to love one another as

Jesus loved us (John 13:34). Isn't that idea more credible than one obsessing over how people behave in the bedroom? After all, disciplinary ideas instruct us how to live. Theological ideas tell us the ways we become truly alive in Christ.

In thinking more about how to develop more authentic and pastoral ministry, I look to Saint Paul. His letters to Christian communities in the New Testament are often directly addressing, if not rebuking, behavior by the faithful. He essentially gave us our first ever textbook in Christian anthropology (for these purposes let's call it the social science looking at the human person and how Christians should behave). But if Christian anthropology has not yet achieved the same cognitive recognition of the *wholeness of the human person*—especially as we consider how human desires drive our actions toward virtue (faith, hope, love, justice, prudence, temperance, and fortitude)—then we need to re-evaluate the way we express it.

One temptation is to simply train people to say no to any behavior that may cause drama. Think of your favorite reality tv show and then consider what the most likely cause of drama is. It's probably a hookup, infidelity, or broken promises. The plotline might focus on a cast member taking a risk based on jealousy, a simple miscalculation, or perhaps even something criminal. And then the unity of the community suffers. People pick sides and someone is cast out. Paul went significantly deeper, looking at the needs of the individual and trying to help them find their path forward in Christian life, not simply avoid the wrong path. In his book dedicated to this topic within moral theology, Greek priest and professor Fr. Basilio Petrà points out that the apostle is a highly pragmatic person. He recognizes that the average Christian of his time needs a spouse to properly control their sexual desires, and conversely the community stringently needs to guard against fulfilling urges through impurities and prostitution (Petrà 2021, 45). What we read in Corinthians is a pastoral plan. Whereas Paul clearly sees celibacy as the highest calling, he understands that it's an unrealistic demand to require of everyone in the Christian communities.

The letters show that Paul is rightfully trying to put a lid on the outrageous pleasure-seeking culture he has heard about in Corinth. Anything that is self-seeking is not seeking God. Through his efforts to build chastity leads Paul to prophetically introduce the Church to a "principle of reality" (Grillo 2022, 114). As in, ideally the Church of his time would prefer everyone choose lifestyle option A (celibacy), but seemingly you are best fit for option B (marriage). What we're missing—or don't clearly understand just from reading the letters—is an awareness that sexuality is a God-given gift to help people relate more fully to one another.

However, even within marriage, we know that the sexual act is not guaranteed to be virtuous. It is possible for two spouses to lust after one another. Yes, even with all the graces that do come within the sacrament of marriage, it is possible for someone to become possessive of the other spouse. And when sex becomes more about "my pleasures" rather than "our pleasures and our relationship" as a committed couple, it fails the essential purpose of being unitive (Petrà 2021, 31).

This is important. If the act of sex is not working toward the unity of the couple—even if a child is born from those relations—it fails to be fully virtuous.

Fertility is another element of pastoral ministry where Christians debate over the term *fruitful*. This subject really tugs at the hearts of couples who want to have a child. Millions of couples privately carry the pain of infertility, with coworkers and friends clueless that they are struggling emotionally. We tend to make fertility a medical issue and that's it. For the countless couples who are not able to conceive, at no fault of their own, that can lead them to feel structurally deficient. Why isn't the body doing what it seemingly was designed to do? Yet their *fruitfulness* can still fully and equally take form in concrete ways through adoption or foster care. Considering the modern world that we live in, understanding the term *bearing fruit* in a wider way than simply giving birth is important for helping people find their Christian path (Fumagalli 2020). So, should we prohibit married couples from sex if they are not able to produce a child for themselves? Of course not, because it is a natural element of God's design that can lead them to strengthen their bond. Their bond helps them be fruitful in many ways. Just as we have to learn how to talk about chastity in ways that teach people how to be alive, we too have to understand that the "fruitfulness" commanded in Genesis is not always a structural or legal term.

You may wonder, have previous generations of Catholics had to grapple with sensitive and complex issues? Yes. Half a century ago many pastors had to draw on the wisdom of the Church to reevaluate its teachings about suicide. This is a difficult topic for many. It used to be a normal part of Catholic discussions about suicide to harp on its sinfulness against the virtue of hope (Barry 1995). Imagine someone tells you the very heavy news that life feels too tough to handle. Do you think reminding them that they are "sinning against hope" would touch their hearts in a transformative way? Probably not. But it's the lack of reaffirming their infinite dignity that would make such a ministry approach fall flat.

As firmly as we continue to hold true that taking one's own life is always wrong, our developed understanding of the human person and psychology has sidelined that argument—not to deny it, but to allow us to focus on what is more relevant.

Despite the ways the Church has caught up on teaching about suicide, we still aren't taking the steps everywhere to make sure those struggling with their sense of self-worth see the parish as a welcoming home. Most individuals suffering to the extent that they end their lives are not in a full state of mind to make rational decisions. And the extremely high rates of suicide among LGBT youth essentially prove that we have not yet figured out a way to put theology into practice for a rather substantial number of individuals.

Pastoral ministry is often practical, reaching people in the deepest part of their heart during a difficult time. Successful pastoral ministry is not restrictionist, as people can sense when we fail to recognize their full dignity—even when they may be struggling with it for themselves.

Thinking of the gay couples in his diocese, in 2014, Doctor of Theology Cardinal Reinhard Marx gave a rather candid response about the work of theologians in this field: "It is not about church doctrine being determined by modern times. It is a question of *aggiornamento*, to say it in a way that the people can understand, and to always adapt our doctrine to the Gospel, to theology, in order to find in a new way the sense of what Jesus said, the meaning of the tradition of the church and of theology and so on. There is a lot to do" (Hansen 2015).

We are increasingly becoming more aware as a Church that there is not simply one singular way to be holy, even in light of the very important virtue of chastity. The awareness that sexual orientation is not a modern fiction has really moved us to go deeper in our understanding of God's design for human relations.

Pastoral ministry began to grapple with sexual orientations more seriously following a 1975 document by the Vatican's doctrine office called *Persona Humana*. It acknowledged that not everyone who is gay is choosing so, even as it upheld that any sexual act must be open to procreation in order to be considered acceptable (Sacred Congregation for Doctrine of the Faith, 1975, VIII). Despite still being very negative toward homosexual persons, it was groundbreaking. What was even more groundbreaking was how the document opened.

The very first sentence says, "The human person is so profoundly affected by sexuality that it must be considered as one of the factors which give to each individual's life the principal traits that distinguish it" (Sacred Congregation for Doctrine of the Faith, 1975). In English-speaking countries, we are very shy about tying sexual orientation to someone's identity. But it is indeed one part of how you, as a whole person, come to understand and interact with the world.

As a general observation, the wider universal Church does not appear to have comprehensively understood how sexuality works (or even agreed on what it is). There are a lot of mixed ideas and approaches to addressing it. Despite claims that we are being consistent, our values develop as we understand the world better. You may have noticed that the way we talk about people who are gay also seems to change decade by decade.

If you were born before the late 1990s, you may have understood homosexuality to be a rebellion or a choice. Then the debate over whether people are born this way took greater hold.

Still very disapproving, many have shifted their argument to say while they no longer think sexual orientation itself is a choice, it becomes a choice to act on it. That statement evokes a lot of conflict within the Christian anthropological thought that theologians have been wrestling with. Critiquing the idea, Fr. Fumagalli said there is a prevailing assumption that because same-sex love doesn't generate (result in a child) that it's only intended purpose must be lust (Fumagalli 2020, 152). But is that true? At the minimum, it is a deeply unsatisfying answer. And to most people, it is interpreted as cruel.

Based on that reasoning, we as a Church have attempted to divorce the way a person was created from how they are inclined to live. We are at an inflection point.

Many cardinals and bishops around the world have already begun to employ a more holistic pastoral practice as it relates to counseling couples. However, particularly in the United States, we continue to open up with a little bit more caution.

My question for Catholic ministry is very simple. Are people leaving our care more empowered or vulnerable? Will they know how to speak out if someone tries to take advantage of them? Can they recognize when someone is minimizing their dignity? Can individuals speak freely, or do we treat their concerns as a liability to the group dynamics?

For people facing difficult and complex family situations, the reality is they may bounce around to various parishes. Even if they are treated well in their immediate home parish, it is not a guarantee the next place is as merciful.

On more than one occasion, I've learned about LGBT individuals who were wholly dedicated to the Catholic faith but despite pouring their hearts and souls into their parish communities could never become anything more than a second-class citizen.

In the 1970s and '80s, some bishops in the United States relied heavily on what was once thought to be sound advice from an expert with a background in both moral theology and psychology. At least at the time, the expert believed people could change their sexual orientation (White 2018). I believe he was genuine, but wrong.

On the delicate topic of abuse, the advice American bishops had received for decades led to some second-guessing as to what punishments for abusers were appropriate. For example, an article in *Crux* states an advisor believed "that priests who sexually abused minors often did so because of sexual addiction, and therefore guilt could not be imputed. On that basis, he claimed bishops could not impose canonical penalties" (White 2018). The reader should note that there is no link between one's sexual orientation and the likelihood to abuse someone.

Considering just how much we have all evolved on this issue in just a matter of decades, it's worth asking again whether there are any gaps. Are we sure that our parishioners have the tools to protect themselves from becoming vulnerable. And are our parishes ready to recognize the full dignity of the individuals we serve, or are we practicing restrictionism?

Unfortunately, I cannot help everyone figure out which specific ministry for LGBT Catholics is the most helpful one for you, if any. The point of this book is to empower people with the tools of discernment—rather than debate Church policies or programs—we need to urgently determine whether someone is more vulnerable to falling victim to abuse (inside, or outside of our parishes) after being told not to proudly accept themselves for how they were made.

As for my personal experiences keeping secrets, it always happened in various parish settings but never as part of any ministry group I participated in. That is why my concerns about vulnerability point to the wider universal Church's record of institutional vice (specifically the global sex abuse scandal) and wonder whether we are genuinely trying to do better.

Imagining that even the best screening practices for hiring employees will never be perfect everywhere, are we placing enough effort into teaching all our youth how to stand up for themselves?

As far as my personal concerns go, it was just a lot of small actions adding up over a decade, and so I rarely questioned the things I was being told in the moment. Instructions not to identify as gay (or being advised that I'm simply experiencing same-sex attraction, but not necessarily gay) led me to hold in all my concerns and anxiety until it could not be held in any longer. Was I naïve?

What if I had the courage to recognize that I was gay, and then publicly identify it. Would anyone in my immediate Catholic circles have listened to me?

I had some experiences as a teenager in a church setting that, as an adult, have made me wonder if lines were crossed. I am not alleging anything criminal or physical, but that the firm reaffirmations of the importance of chastity and sinfulness of gay lifestyles heightened an environment, where as a minor, I was already less equipped to recognize where the boundaries might be. Years later, there was a priest elsewhere who privately insisted that I avoid telling others—including other priests—about my sexuality. The shame I experienced, internalized, and attempted to hide for years was overwhelming. Imagine thinking because of what individuals had told you, that you are so broken that you cannot even tell other priests in Confession. Believe it or not, at the time it was extremely comforting. If it was that terrible of a secret, I thought I'd never have to come out to my parents. I'd never have to face the whole truth.

Facing the whole truth is hard. But after all, the truth is what we as Catholics are claiming to preach.

And then, the news about Cardinal McCarrick and his alleged abuses became public. I thought, wait a minute? Have I been holding in secrets at my own expense? Even if the advice I was offered was genuine. Was it bad advice?

Seemingly, as soon as I spoke up publicly and said something, the default answer from several Catholics over and over was, "Can I introduce you to a group meeting for people with same-sex attraction?" I think they wanted to be helpful, but I did not take anyone up on their offer. One priest, after hearing about what I had gone through, reaffirmed to me "the Church was calling me to heroic chastity."

I'm in full agreement that heroic chastity is a good ideal!

But for me, this was not great advice. Thinking back to earlier examples of the Church reworking its pastoral care of those with mental illness, as an institution we used to try and offer simple clarity. Considering suicide? That's wrong…a sin against hope!

Clear advice is not always helpful advice. I wanted people to hear my pain and recognize my inherent dignity as a person. Successful pastoral ministry means reaching people, with all of their pains and fortified walls, in the deepest part of their hearts.

I have often felt that in seeking counsel, the tables were flipped to focus on my sinfulness, and that for some, we just never got around to questions about whether the ministry and advice I received was appropriate or helpful. Where was the outrage or responsibility? Where is the urgency to address my concerns?

After coming out, I lost some friends. "We love you, but." The restrictionism attitude led several people to feel that despite knowing my heart and my dignity for many years, there was an uncomfortable idea that hanging out with me and supporting me might jeopardize their own standing with the Church.

I share these things not to encourage anyone to feel bitter, but so you know that in speaking up about reality, you will slowly help unwind a longstanding culture of silence. While I think the intentions of those who told me to keep quite about my desires were well meaning, for me, it was unhelpful and bad advice.

Successful pastoral ministry happens when dignity and moral theology are fully integrated. Instead of a framework of discipline and ordered rules, the chaos in our lives must be transformed into something that is fully alive. Something transcendent, that speaks to the uniqueness and value God sees in the person we are counseling.

As part of the Catholic Church's efforts to reconcile with the countless victims of spiritual and physical abuse, the bishops should launch a full review to assess if we are widely using sound psychology for the present day. Or if we are even remaining true to the 1975 Vatican declaration that says sexuality is an exceptionally critical element of someone's identity? To the extent that a review of procedures and support mechanisms authentically confirms or challenges us to address pastoral practices, we should expect action to be taken.

I have faith that we will get to a time when everyone's infinite dignity is recognized and not relegated to wait outside the church.

The delicate issue of pastoral ministry for LGBT Catholics has innumerable different approaches. It reflects how the Church's understanding of the issue is rapidly changing. And, probably shows how this is not a one size fits all.

The idea that the natural variants of human sexuality exist along a spectrum and are not a choice is a rather startling complexity to have to reconcile with old ideas. But a rather significant number of Cardinals and nearly a consensus of moral theologians have accepted that things are more complex than we used to assume. Cardinal Jean-Claude Hollerich, a theologian from Luxembourg and member of the Holy Father's inner council, famously shared his perspective that "the sociological-scientific foundation of this teaching [on homosexuality] is no longer correct, what one formerly condemned was sodomy" (Caldwell 2022).

Some scholars have argued that "natural" corresponds to how God created the person, and its morality can be judged by whether those gifts are freely returned with authentic love and with justice (Lawler and Salzman 2022).

Professor Keenan reminds us that for a proper moral judgment to take place, we must look at the entire picture. We cannot cherry-pick a particular element of the thing we are trying to judge. And as stated earlier, moral theologians are charged with minimizing what is wrong in all our actions. Even the best-case scenario must be played out in the context of an imperfect world, and consequently every moral action is at least a tiny bit deficient (Selling 2016, 77). Does the fact that something is partially deficient mean that it is immoral? No. Otherwise even your best efforts and greatest work would be immoral. That simply isn't reality.

The Church says that the ideal relationship is one man and one woman united through the sacrament of marriage. Re-stating what was said earlier by Monsignor Philippe Bordeyne, "Let's be realistic: not all people who cannot marry have the capacity to live alone. Are they not entitled to the support of the Church on their journey of faith and conversion?" (Houdaille 2022).

Like Saint Paul, the Church may prefer you live a life alone. But perhaps based on how God designed you, you are better suited for something different.

For some theologians, that is exactly what they view as the next step in developing our teachings on human sexuality. They wonder if we must focus on those elements: gifts that are freely given with just and authentic love. For example, in 2015, Doctor of Theology Cardinal Christoph Schönborn spoke about a faithful gay couple he knows:

> It's an improvement. They share a life, they share their joys and sufferings, they help one another. It must be recognized that this person took an important step for his own good and the good of others, even though it certainly is not a situation the Church can consider "regular." (Wooden 2015)

These "unique" situations are increasingly coming out into the open, making it obvious that LGBT relationships are not uncommon and that stable, healthy relationships are preferable to unstable ones.

Once we know about the pastoral crises and demands the Church is facing, theologians then get to work helping the Holy

Father and our bishops communicate the revealed truths of the faith for emerging problems. Truth is never invented out of thin air, nor does it oppose the core realities that have been preached before. Even if we did not have the vocabulary centuries ago to describe the problems facing us now, moral theologians would say Catholic teaching must stay faithful to those essential core realities accepted by Catholics everywhere and always. That is all a very long way of saying stay true to "sacred tradition" as it was passed down to us.

If pastoral care is not ready to tackle all of the challenges the modern world has thrown at it, it likely just means that our Church needs to go deeper in its own relationship to the risen Christ. And remaining close to sacred tradition, we also turn to divine revelation in the Bible to ensure that we are equally as faithful but also looking for the things we may have missed.

Understanding Biblical Context

Moral theology and conscience are always bound by scripture. Throughout history, the Church has had to wrestle with competing visions of the Bible's message. What are Catholics supposed to take away from this? Well, the message of the Gospel can be summed up as: God is love, mercy, and seeks to reconcile all people to his loving embrace.

Vatican theologians controversially wrote an opinion that the Old Testament makes no mention of people who are gay. None. Their opinion stated that the famous story of Sodom and Gomorrah fits into the Abraham cycle of blessings and curses, danger and deliverance (Pontifical Biblical Commission 2019). The insinuation is that in the story, a vulnerable guest—whom God expected the people of Sodom and Gomorrah to welcome and protect—faced dominances and gross acts of aggression.

The same Vatican report could be used to offer caution for gay Catholics. It notes that the Book of Leviticus includes homosexual acts among a list of prohibited behaviors (Pontifical Biblical Commission 2019). What are they referring to? While that is anything but a green light for LGBT individuals, it raises the question of whether it's appropriate to continue using stories like Sodom and Gomorrah out of context. Even more difficult is trying to discern what the right context is.

Biblical scholar Jeffrey Siker also verified that the early Christians had no concept of homosexuality as we understand it today. He noted that acts that would fall under the category of sex, particularly between males (females not specified), were condemned, but that they were condemned—without any context—side by side with many other rules that Christians consider to be completely archaic, like not cutting your hair at the temples. He and the host, Dr. Bart Ehrman, wrestled with how to judge one of the rules in Leviticus 19 as more important than others or if we simply think of all of them as irrelevant in Christianity. Throw it all out? Probably not. Jesus was himself a faithful Jew and stated that he did not come to abolish the law (Siker 2023).

There is, however, plenty of evidence in that Jesus wanted the Jews to understand the greater meaning behind the law. It is worth considering whether Jesus really hated the religious leaders of his time as much as we have let ourselves believe. Some thinkers affiliated with the Vatican have even speculated that maybe the scribes and the Pharisees had more in common with Jesus than we care to admit. Fr. Di Luccio and Fr. Grilli, both who have served as professors of theology at Gregorian University in Rome, commented on this stating, "Trust in God, judgment, faith in the resurrection, the expectation of future fulfilment and so on belong both to the foundations of rabbinical Judaism and to those of Christianity. Reading some Gospel pages, one could even assume that Jesus was a Pharisee" (Di Luccio and Grilli 2019).

Why, then, are there nearly one hundred references to the Pharisees in the New Testament? What is the greater meaning that Jesus was trying to get us to understand? One perspective is that Jesus wanted his community to mature: to move beyond understanding their relationship with God as a list of rules and obligations, and instead seek God through the foundations of love. After all, Jesus Christ freely sacrificed himself in the greatest act of love on the cross for the sake of justice.

The writings of St. Paul in the New Testament help shed some light on the maturity we should be seeking. Paul addressed his letters to entire communities of Christians like the Corinthians, the Galatians, the Romans, and so on. Biblical scholar Dr. Wayne Meeks said Paul was seeking to fortify the communities as a whole, which helps us understand his view of ethics and morals (Keenan 2022, 29). We are not pagans, and so our lives should not look like those of the pagans. Instead, St. Paul stresses the importance of moral growth, both as individuals and collectively as communities (Keenan 2022, 29). Whatever the case, the Bible does not condone lust and always encourages relationships with strong fidelity to the other.

Means of Authentic Development in Doctrine

As stated at the beginning of this chapter, for any reader who would like to verify the following perspectives on doctrinal development for themselves, I recommend searching online for "L'evoluzione della dottrina spiegata da 'Civiltà Cattolica'" (The evolution of doctrine explained) by Andrea Tornielli in *La Stampa* in 2016. This archive is a freely accessible version of La Civiltà Cattolica's perspective, a publication that is edited by the Vatican Secretariat of State.

Catholicism is remarkably exciting in the sense that it is alive! It is open to new possibilities so long as they reflect reality, conform to the truths that have been believed everywhere and always, and do not contradict divine revelation. Unwanted Catholics can take special solace in the fact they are indeed wanted by Christ.

This section will review what theologians have said about how doctrine develops—to keep it in mind as you pray and discern your own God-given identity (which is still not a chosen identity, but one that reflects God's creativity)—because they understand the way moral theologians are increasingly approaching this difficult subject.

Unfortunately it is impossible to speak to every situation that readers may be seeking answers to. But I hope this can at least help you on your path to healing.

This book chooses to say that theology "develops" instead of "evolves." Our faith is not like a Pokémon that levels up and becomes something else. But even when we say some teachings are set in stone, it's not as though the entire stone tablet has been filled. We are learning and maturing, and theology will only become more beautiful over time—like a budding rose.

This book does not call for a change in doctrine. Doctrine should never be part of a political campaign. This book advocates for the reader to reflect on their own place in God's creation, to reflect on what virtue looks like in their own life, to seek authenticity before God, and be in union with the magisterium (the teaching authority of the Church).

Thankfully, the process of developing doctrine does not always have to be painful. Pope Francis said that St. Vincent's "happy formulation" that Christian doctrine is "consolidated by years, enlarged by time, [and] refined by age" is a "very clear and illuminating" rule for proper doctrinal development (Francis 2017).

Authentic theology does not feel threatened by science but sees it as a companion in discovering the ultimate reality, which we call God. Even as many moral theologians feel that the Church may be ready for an authentic development in doctrine today, the magisterium wisely goes slowly to make sure we are stating the reality of God's design for humans to the best extent possible, and to make sure that we can link arms as Catholics and walk together. Cardinal Tobin said in 2019, "A rethinking of the mystery of human sexuality is important, is incumbent. It's not going to be done in a weekend.

But I think we have to be able to ask questions of each other as we go forward" (Tobin 2019).

Changes are inevitable. They are a sign of growth and that we are still alive. We will stop growing when we die. For this reason we have to pray and support the moral theologians of the Church so that future developments advance, and not corrupt doctrine. The next section will explore some of the ways theologians think about developments.

This section will very briefly explain three methods of development:

1. Sharpening a grainy image
2. Maturing
3. Balancing

FIRST METHOD: SHARPENING A GRAINY IMAGE

A doctor of canon law (a church lawyer) was talking with me about human sexuality and said, "The doctrine is [already] clear." Maybe he had hoped that would end our conversation.

From a disciplinary standpoint, he is right. However, Doctor of Theology Cardinal Reinhard Marx famously said, "I am astonished that some can say, 'Everything is clear' on this topic. Things are not clear" (Hansen 2015).

I don't think the cardinal meant to be funny when he said that things are not clear. After all, when we are talking about human sexuality, we are largely using terms that were completely unknown a century ago. And if we don't have agreed-upon terminology, or have already thrown out some of the underlying psychology the Church relied on a few decades ago, then we have some work to do.

Forty years ago, it is possible that many disciplinarians simply adopted the most satisfying explanation of human sexuality that was available at the time. Maybe we did not know that the definitions and assumptions we had about the complexity of the human person were very grainy images. Thank goodness, the scientists and psychologists did not stop researching. Things are clearer now.

I remember wondering about the universe in high school religion class. The early tribes of Israel believed that there was a massive dome in the sky and that there were waters above it. And occasionally, the deep blue seas above us would leak through and give us rain. And then I remembered from science class that the Hubble Telescope was pointed at an empty patch of seemingly dark sky, ultimately to discover a few thousand galaxies. Wow! We have come a long way.

Have we finished discovering? Is that the end of our human capacities to understand the world God created? Or if we keep trying, would we eventually see the invisible God himself? If you look at the James Webb Space Telescope images from 2022, it gives you pause because of how our stunning technological advances can make things clear. I didn't even realize before that some of the previous images were grainy, and now I wonder if they are as clear and sharp as they will ever be, or if science will prove something magical yet again.

Theology is not that different. In this case, the key is discerning if a development is analogical (similar) and has continuity. It can't be something totally new. It can't say the new telescope images suddenly don't see the galaxies Hubble discovered decades ago. That wouldn't make any sense and wouldn't reflect reality.

In terms of theology, this means examining how the context, not the content, has changed. It's not so much that the original idea was wrong, as the core truth that some masses or bodies of stars exist where Hubble Deep Field is looking will forever remain true. But as we have better and more reliable information, it necessitates a change in the way we teach and relate that truth.

As it relates to human sexuality, we now have enough knowledge of the human person to know that this is a complex subject. In the United States especially, I'd be curious to see how an increased cultural awareness and openness—and ever-increasing presence of monogamous gay families—has led us to a clearer picture. In 2005, an assessment of "deep-seated homosexuality" included, "Strong physical attraction is present to other men's bodies and to the masculinity of others due to profound weakness in male confidence" (Fitzgibbons 2005). From my personal reflection, there were certain parts of me that felt unconfident because I was keeping secrets about my desires and sexuality. But it is not clear how one assesses it as a cause of homosexuality. A lot has changed since 2005. But as far as preaching truth, more well-collected data is always better. It would not be unusual in a scientific setting for earlier images from a telescope to be grainy.

It only makes sense that we revisit the data to see if we understand ourselves better, to see if the image is clearer and sharper than in previous decades.

SECOND METHOD: MATURING

Think of all the qualities involved in researching and developing a new technology or a new medicine. It takes an understanding of lessons learned from past experiments, requires some level of personal risk, and involves processes of innovation. Authentic science doesn't try to reinvent the wheel; it has a keen respect what is generally already held to be true. By the methods scientists use, you can usually tell if they value the dignity of the people they are trying to affect, or if their work is motivated by greed or superiority. Ultimately, if successful, the risks that science takes can improve the quality of life for humankind.

Likewise, if we think of the Church as a father to the people of God, then we can also contemplate how the risks our own parents encouraged us to take as kids helped us mature. Parents inevitably decide on the level of sheltering vs. exposure to the world on our journey to becoming great men and women. As we dig into just how theology *matures*, think of a baby who eventually grows up to become an adolescent, and even later an adult. St. Vincent de Lérins was creative and maintained that the essence remains of the original, although at each stage, the person looks different (Guarino 2018, 21). This approach is vital to mature theology too.

But people have come to expect and even want an aversion to risk in their church. Church for many becomes a safety net in an otherwise unhinged world. An international student once told me that she enrolled in a Catholic university because, as a foreign student, she wanted to be somewhere the administrators and professors would discipline her if she started to go off track in her studies, or if her social life became too wild. She wanted to feel safe, and that is a completely valid desire. Yet, in the field of theology, providing people with a sense of security is not the mission of the Church. Rather we're called to help people mature in their faith and equip the faithful in tackling tough issues for themselves.

The fear—and anxiety—of taking risks is one of the main reasons theology stalls. Without this, theology turns away from its purpose of discovering God and becomes a stale discipline. Rather, when it is functioning at its best, it works closely with canon lawyers to help people realize the grace of salvation. For too long we have attempted to overexplain disciplines to provide people a sense of security and keep them safe from sin.

Reality is not as clean and clear-cut as we have made it out to be. For example, the extremely important topic of *virtues* was slowly separated after the seventeeth century in the study of natural law as it relates to sexuality (Keenan 2022, 218). That stunted our spiritual growth and perhaps knocked theology off track for centuries. During a speech to moral theologians in Rome, Pope Francis countered this by reminding, "Theologians are called to explore the connections between grace and freedom, virtues and laws, and the plurality of languages and the uniqueness of *agape* (love)" (Watkins 2022).

As moral theology helps the Church mature by re-focusing the idea of human relations, human fraternity, and even sexuality grounded solidly in the virtues of faith, hope, love, justice, and so on, we start to see how everyone has unique responsibilities toward one another. Moral theology tries to help the faithful limit bad consequences while attempting to maximize the common good. We discussed earlier how the Ten Commandments were initially thought of as rules for community life. In this area, moral theology tends to focus less on sins and instead on finding the best way to help us relate to one another as God created us. "I give you a new commandment, that you love one another. Just as I have loved you, you also should love one another" (John 13:34). It's about building relationships on a solid foundation of love and mutual growth—a path to holiness.

Now apply the theological approach of *maturing* to technology. Consider how each individual step in creating the cell phone was considered revolutionary and advanced for its time. There was so much risk involved in creating the telephone. Consider the electricity, ugly wires, education, and cost involved in getting a telephone in every house. People were skeptical, and at times even afraid of where this technology would bring us.

Imagine trying to send a telegraph through Morse code. What did sending a message look, sound, and feel like? *Tap. Tap tap. Tap tap tap.* This was the modern-day smartphone in its infancy.

(Embryonic) The telegraph key conveys Morse code
(Infancy) Box telephone
(Toddler) Telephone switchboard
(Adolescent) "Brick" cell phone
(Adult) Smartphone
(Senior) To be determined

Yet, at the same time, I can't help but notice that the telegraph key seems more similar to my everyday use of the phone in 2023 (text messaging) than all of the intermediary inventions that took place between. The functions, communication methods, and the form all look different. The core purpose of communication remains the same.

Looking for overlapping ideas and similarities has been key to the work of many ethicists. More than four decades ago, James Nelson wanted to help Christians move away from a dualistic mindset and instead understand that sexual sins happen when the body becomes an object, either out of fear or treated as pleasure (Larkman 2015).

Faithful to the theology of Augustine, Professor Grillo says the job of theologians is to hold up evidence and reason, and help the Church delicately navigate the findings so that it can speak authoritatively. He says, "What is asked of us today is not simply to replace the words of tradition with new words, but to offer an interpretation that accounts for the forms of life and of the evidence which more men and women today orient their sexual life of encounter and communion" (Grillo 2022, 33).

There are two important terms that theologians have proposed the Church help mature: *complementarity* and *fecundity* (fruitfulness). Listen to the words of Fr. Aristide Fumagalli at the Archdiocesan Seminary of Milan: "The condemnation of homosexual acts does not contemplate the possibility, unknown until contemporary times, that homosexual acts correspond to the nature of the person and express personal love.... Therefore not acts dictated by 'religious idolatry and hedonistic selfishness'—the two conditions that make them unacceptable—but expression of personal Christian love" (Moia 2020). His book *L'amore possibile* lays out a convincing and thorough case for the Church to continue developing its theology on sexuality in more meaningful and deep ways, rather than solely examining how body parts exchange and fit.

According to the professor, the assumed purpose of sexuality already began to be balanced out following Vatican Council I, where it was no longer just about procreative fertility but also "a personal communion of the two spouses" (Fumagalli 2020, 159). For Catholics, sex is a gift by God for two purposes: *procreative* and *unitive.* Thus, the problem for gay couples is they lack a structural difference that would allow them to be fruitful and multiply. But despite our assurances that these acts bring forth a beautiful personal union between the two spouses, so far Church law focuses on the structural side of things (the exchange of body parts). Sexuality is so much more than that! Without discounting the limits of Catholic theology for same-sex couples (and the issue of sexual otherness is unlikely to ever be resolved), how will the Church compensate in the decades to come by contemplating more deeply the unitive and relational properties of sex?

The Church made further steps forward by adopting a more analogical style of thinking (looking at how things are similar, not just how they are different) during Vatican II. Over time we could also adopt a more mature approach to defining LGBT issues by trying to understand them for what they are. In other words, if we limit our understandings of sexuality to just the structural elements, we will never be able to fully understand the unitive properties. Does looking at the term *fruitfulness* solely in a structural sense make sense in a spiritual or relational capacity? Or does our understanding of term *fruitfulness* need further maturity, capable of helping all couples reach the heights of responsible love in personal communion with one another (Fumagalli 2020, 174)?

Just as the apostles were horrified their teacher Jesus saw the woman at the well (a woman many people only think of because of her many failed relationships), it's a reminder that even those we initially dismiss as deficient also have important gifts to offer. That is why Jesus called her to be the first non-Jewish missionary. Perhaps Jesus is asking us to mature enough to see the innate value and gifts of same-sex couples and the often-misjudged love that couples offer their communities.

THIRD METHOD: BALANCING OUT

Sometimes, new and better information helps us understand that our existing teachings are still true, but maybe they were presented in a way that was overwhelmingly one-sided. This method of doctrine development isn't totally dissimilar from the maturing we just explored together in the last section.

Imagine ordering your favorite meal at a restaurant. The waiter repeats back to you what you asked for, just to confirm it was correct.

You hear them say "a basket of fries" and quickly say, "No! I asked for a burger and a side of fries." The waiter repeats again, "A basket of fries!" It's a silly example, but sometimes for unknown reasons we all become fixated on one small part of the whole.

This can happen for a variety of reasons. Maybe we left information out because it didn't seem important at the time, and now shifts in culture are forcing us to explain why we ignored certain data. Or further research on a topic has led us to learn that both options A and B can be true at the same time.

As mentioned in the previous section on *maturing* theology, Vatican II sought to help the Church move away from the trap of only thinking about how things are different. Theologian Karl Rahner, in particular, was influential in steering theology to something more mature, moving beyond dialectical thinking (looking at contradictions and conflict) to something more analogical (searching for similarities). After all the time we have spent listing the reasons that straight and gay people are different, it would be immature not to look for the similarities. "Rahner tried to free us from a strict, dualistic mindset that saw everything as composed of two, often opposing, parts: grace and nature, divine and human, soul and body, church, and world. Rahner saw connections, not separations; unity, not division" (O'Brien 2004).

Sacramental theologian Dr. Andrea Grillo says that a recalibration of Church positions has happened several times throughout history. On the theme of sexuality, he noted that equating certain sexual acts as intrinsically evil appears too absolutist (Grillo 2020). Particularly in theology, which is rarely strictly black and white, absolutism can be a marker that someone is part of a social pact or a political group.

Here is another example. The Church used to prohibit the burial of suicide victims in Catholic cemeteries to highlight the wrongness and impermissibility of killing oneself. Psychology was able to later clarify that there are grave psychological conditions that likely lessen the culpability of suicide. Therefore, theology was able to develop to reflect an openness to mercy.

You might say that was a pastoral change (the approach we use to serve people in difficult situations) and not a change in teaching. That's correct in a sense. The balancing of the doctrine happened as we shifted the focus away from "sin against hope" to our newfound call to communion with one another.

As the papal encyclical *Fratelli Tutti* says, "Life exists where there is bonding, communion, fraternity; and life is stronger than death when it is built on true relationships and bonds of fidelity. On the contrary, there is no life when we claim to be self-sufficient and live as islands: in these attitudes, death prevails" (Francis 2020).

As noted earlier, our Church relied for several decades on what turned out to be extremely unfortunate advice from psychologists on human sexuality and sex abuse. As a result we should not be afraid to completely revisit what we know about the human person and how we relate to one another. A "balancing" of wisdom does not require challenging the sacramental understanding of marriage (the union before God that the Church considers the highest type of relationship between one man and one woman).

We also should not fall into the trap of throwing out all that is old. Instead, we should inspect where there are differences and determine if they need our attention. Professor Grillo talks about St. Thomas Aquinas and the *principle of indeterminacy of the particular*. In other words, "it seems that the natural law is not the same for everyone" (Grillo 2022, 147). Aquinas seemed comfortable with the tension between occasional theology and disciplinary practices. He understood wisdom to be virtue of balance between applying lessons learned from the past and allowing enough freedom to negotiate new problems (Calogero 1994, 176).

The extremely important and consequential document by Pope Paul VI on human sexuality in 1965, *Humanae Vitae*, affirms the twofold *procreative* and *unitive* purposes of sex. But the document spends all its energy focusing on social issues that cause harm to the procreative side of things. Even in natural family planning, the Church allows couples to enjoy sex at the moments where the possibility of fertility is at its lowest, thus highlighting the need to be balanced and also think about sex and its unitive purposes (Fumagalli 2023, 160–61).

In fact, a future balancing out of Catholic doctrine on complementarity and fruitfulness could also be used to help highlight the sacredness of the sacrament of marriage. The sacrament—which is limited to one man and one woman—is the only type of relationship that theology would state has the complete set of tools in the toolbox (structural, generative, relational, spiritual, etc.)

By reevaluating the terms that describe unitive and relational benefits of others living in communion (even nonsexual), in the theological sense, many types of relationships allow people to flourish. For example, the Church could decide to shower blessings on many types of relationships that exist out there (community homes for widows and widowers, siblings, same-sex partners, and married partners). In a world plagued by loneliness and isolation, each type of relationship listed above offers ways for people to flourish in community. By thinking of more ways and situations in which the Church could bless people living in communion, our priests would not be offering legal declarations about how incredible one relationship is over another. No. A blessing helps remind us of the importance of building up virtue and living out responsibility in communion with others.

Although it's tempting, it's worth the reminder that in thinking about sex, we should think of the unitive properties in relationships as mutual grounding of our lives in faith, hope, charity, and justice. And then, only after that, come to understand that the diversity in the ways that people relate to one another further emphasizes just how special the procreative possibilities are between one man and one woman.

There are many types of unions, ways that people relate to one another to form bonds, create positivity, and introduce stability into their lives. The Church can recognize these various ways while still underlining how special the sacrament is.

THE BELGIUM MODEL

As a bishop's conference, these bishops are among the top trained in theology in the world. For decades, they have observed problems with how some groups try to marginalize certain Catholics, and ultimately decided to act. The bishops of Belgium decided they should lean on the Church's already existing knowledge of theology to help shift the pastoral strategy somewhere more productive. The debates weren't loud or garnering the attention of international media like those of other bishops conferences. No, they wanted to avoid politicizing this sensitive topic and instead focus their efforts in support of LGBT couples who are making lifelong decisions for themselves. If couples are making commitments that are generally positive, stabilizing, and permanent—even if they do not comport with Catholic disciplinary practices—it is something we should seek to place in a Christian context.

In Belgium, the Church decided to take couples who give themselves freely to one another, according to their own capabilities, and help them see how their love can correspond to Christian love, and to know that it is possible even when the conditions of their love do not amount to the *sacrament* of marriage. After all, we can recognize virtue wherever it is growing.

This is extremely refreshing!

To understand a sense of just how great this feels, I compare it to commentary I had heard when I was younger that told me that gay people feel a natural sense of shame and want public approval to help alleviate their shame. And once, in Confession at a parish I was just visiting, the counsel I received was that my love is only an imitation of the love that people in the sacrament of marriage experience.

Yet, instead of focusing on what is negative, I encourage my fellow Catholics to focus on the reasons for hope.

It is time to set aside the language of secrecy.

It is time for us to try something new. Something more authentic!

Monsignor Philippe Bordeyne, theologian and President of the John Paul II Institute for Marriage and Family Sciences (a Vatican-backed university), had a very candid moment with Catholic reporters in 2022. He said, "Let's be realistic: not all people who cannot marry have the capacity to live alone. Are they not entitled to the support of the Church on their journey of faith and conversion? We must dare to be pastorally creative" (Houdaille 2022).

As Pope Francis was quoted earlier in this book, the world exists in many shades of gray rather than black and white. This is why the Church must become better at discerning so that priests and other ministers can learn how to apply teachings in a way that is relevant to the Christians seeking their advice.

It's a recognition that the true meaning of love becomes clearer when individuals boldly take responsibility for another person. Not in a possessive way, but in one that upholds their full dignity. Even if doctrine right now finds someone's relationship imperfect, we should still as a general principle encourage commitment, permanence, and stability. Those can lead one to more virtue.

When we allow people to live as they were made and encourage them to make stabilizing and positive decisions for themselves, the outcomes are certainly much healthier. On the other hand, living in the closet can lead to spiritual illness and even physical too. The Church has to develop a way to help people find these paths to a positive life.

That is why I want to shift attention to the Belgium Model, where the Catholic bishops in charge of each diocese have attained doctorates of theology. They are attuned carefully to ways we can help people become the best disciples of Jesus Christ they can be and to move the Church from a place of discipline to a community of love rooted in the Gospel.

These bishops are not seeking to overturn doctrine, but instead offer people an authentic way of living that is structured and tethered to the Catholic people.

That is why, after having informed the Vatican and Pope Francis of their unanimous desire to launch an experiment giving gay couples an anchor in Christian life, the Flemish-speaking dioceses of Belgium began offering blessings to long-term committed gay couples in 2022. Theologian Jos Moons commented, "The Flemish bishops have made it their priority to opt for inclusion and conscience. That is a valid Catholic position" (Moons 2022).

Professor Andrea Grillo thinks about this as the Church's ability to recognize the "possible good" of same-sex couples (Grillo 2022). In other words, if a relationship promotes stability and contributes to the common good of society, then there is at least some limited area where the Church can and should encourage people on their path. Theology cannot exist in a vacuum; it must have practical implications on the lives of the people—even those in difficult circumstances.

The bishops have proven not only that it is possible to do this without a change in doctrine, but that it is something pastorally important.

I invite you to dare imagine yourself and your partner walking into a Catholic Church holding hands, nervously approaching the Blessed Sacrament, and asking God to guide you in unchartered territory. This is an act of faith and hope.

After reading from scripture, but without exchanging rings, the already civilly united couple proclaims their thanksgiving to God and asks for divine help, as two people striving to live faithfully as two people seeking the nearness of God.

The priest gathers his hands in prayer as he says the following over the gay couple:

> *God and Father, we surround N. and N. with our prayer today. You know their heart and the way they will go together from now on. Make their commitment to each other strong and faithful. Let their house be filled with understanding, tolerance, and care. Let there be room for reconciliation and*

peace. Let the love they share be their joy and serve them in our community.

Give us the strength to go with them, together in the footsteps of your Son, and strengthened by your Spirit. (Flemish-Speaking Bishops Conference of Belgium 2022)

With this blessing, each member of the couple takes on the responsibility of walking as a child of God. To recognize that you were created in God's image, are a reflection of divine creativity, and that you are able to relate to a partner in a committed relationship is a recognition of your complementarity. It is a reminder that you are meant to live in communion with others, especially those who are different and even mean to you. And when people do not offer you the love and peace of Christ, you are to freely offer it to them anyway.

The Belgium Model is especially refreshing because it is being implemented without a spirit of "activism." You may recall that the German bishops have mainly authorized the identical thing as Belgium, yet the lead up to the Synodal Way felt coordinated—whether it was or not—and as a result many people wonder if politics got in the way of the Holy Spirit. Who am I to say?

On the other hand, in Belgium, the bishops worked to keep the Vatican in the loop during every step of the process. They spoke in unison (easier to do since there are fewer bishops than in Germany) and told the Holy Father that this was their desire.

Theology is an expression of reality. Which also means that it is not an expression of politics. We must trust in the Holy Spirit to guide us organically.

My hope is that the Catholic Church will find a way to accompany LGBT couples in every country in a spirit of justice and charity that fully reflects reality and serves the whole human person.

CONCLUSION

THIS BOOK HAS reflected on scripture, discernment, and what the moral theologians of today are saying. All three of these should lead us to think, "I need to mature." It doesn't matter if you are the greatest theologian or a Christian embarking on their first day of studying the faith. We have room to mature, but we cannot do it by ourselves. We need the Holy Spirit.

At the great feast of Pentecost, the Holy Spirit roared through locked doors and made the apostles speak in languages they never thought possible. The Holy Spirit enabled them to communicate with the nations in a way that edified God's design for creation as one. The apostles could never have done this on their own.

Their eyes were opened to see Christianity's relationship to peoples of every background and to understand the beauty of diversity according to God's design for humankind.

Once they were able to understand "the other" they were no longer afraid to go out and preach the Gospel. At each step in Christian history, we have been drawn to gradually see the world in a more enlightened way that continues to surprise people.

In today's day and age, you wouldn't be surprised seeing news stories featuring the great gifts and talents of individuals with disabilities. That way of thinking did not make sense in the Middle Ages because the dignity of the human person—even though it was proclaimed as universal—was understood in somewhat of a privileged way. This applied to adopted children, women, and those born outside of a marriage as well. Rather than thinking God would have made them differently if he really wanted them to have authority, today it's abundantly clear each person is made unique and in the image of God. Each of us has gifts, but that understanding of the world took time.

So many people have been told in error that their mere existence, because of their personal traits, conflicts with the law. As recalled earlier, I kept secrets about my desires because I thought that would allow everything to be okay. I had heard commentary in a Catholic setting that said people identity their sexuality to alleviate a sense of shame. And in confession at a parish I was visiting, I had been told that my love is only an imitation. That prompted me to keep the lid on my own identity for many years and try to hide from God. But today, I declare that the language of secrecy and abuse is dead.

Today is a new day! A day to be authentic before the God who made me!

Your sexuality is a gift from God. Strive to orient your life and your relationships to the reality you were designed for, with special attention toward faith, hope, charity, and justice.

For the "unwanted" Catholic, the path to freedom and confidence in your identity can be found in Catholic theology. Theology is like the new telescope that makes us realize just how grainy the previous images of galaxies actually are. It doesn't overturn or replace the knowledge that the old telescope produced, instead, it compliments it by making everything much more clear.

The "natural law" too is sufficiently flexible enough to be able to explain your reality and the way God created you. You were created in God's image and that is more than good!

In this book, you have learned that the natural law must be fully re-integrated to virtues and discernment if we want to live the most authentic life that God created us for. And that we have to spend a lot of time working on that path to holiness, and less time looking inward. This includes orienting our sexual lives to the way

God created us. And through the differences in sexuality, we have learned that God has created more than one way to seek communion with others in his creation.

Acts of Faith: If we go back only seventy-five years, there were many Catholic parishes that were segregated in the United States. The rejection of "the other" was often enforced by the congregations themselves, that in practice did not recognize that God made everyone in his image. Yet, the acts of faith by Black Catholics heroically helped many people of different backgrounds mature in their theology. LGBT Catholics also need to accept the graces offered by faith that makes you proudly declare, "I am made by God. I am unique in my abilities and my gifts. And I declare that all of me is made for the Lord as he intended."

Hope: I am created in the image of God. No one else has ever been created with my exact experiences in life. My sexuality is included as an immutable (unchanging) part of who I am. How do I live a life that orients this toward God? Through an act of hope, which is done through giving our trust and confidence to another. And to give ourselves in a way that helps the other person become better. In the theological sense, each of us is called to live our lives as a mirror of the love Jesus Christ has for each one of us, in the hope that together we attain the greatest happiness in the life to come.

Love: I must seek the best for others, so that we can live eternally in communion with God. Our experiences, our gifts, and the areas we lack all reveal a vast array of ways in which God has designed us to need "the other." We are most fulfilled in our natural lives when we freely give ourselves, instead of reflecting on what we can keep for ourselves. This is sometimes most easily seen at a soup kitchen, where seemingly one Christian is presenting his or her gift to the other. But really, we need the experience of the person living in poverty almost more than they need the food being handed out because their experiences and identity are gifts that help us understand a more complete picture of God's creation. Our sexuality is one component of the way we relate freely to others.

Justice: If theology is reality, it is also a lived experience. I must reflect on the life that God gave me, not the one I would have chosen for myself. And I must live it in the most authentic way possible. My sexuality is not to be understood as a God-given evil, but as a gift. And gifts are made to be freely and completely given to others. In the past, we thought that LGBT people chose their sexuality in rebellion. That poverty of understanding has been enlightened by lived experience and by the vastly improved work by the moral theologians of today. We are to maximize the good we can do, minimize the wrong, and walk confidently knowing that we are made in the image of God.

And when others fail to recognize your dignity and the responsibility you bring with you to the Church, turn to scripture. Recognizing the way Jesus waited for the woman at the well (John 4), and asked her for her gift of water, I too know that I have something of value to give to the Church. It is time for you too to be a prophetic voice celebrating the unique way in which God designed you, and your ability to relate to the rest of God's creation.

And while this book has given an overview of what most moral theologians of today's day and age are saying, the most important thing to remember is that theology is simply reality. Theology is not a means for discipline and it cannot be owned or possessed.

Theology is reality. And if it is reality, then you must be living it!

Let's close with the words Jesus said during his first sermon when his own fellow religious friends in Nazareth rejected him; let's pray together:

The Spirit of the Lord is upon me, because he has anointed me to preach good news to the poor. He has sent me to proclaim release to the captives and recovering of sight to the blind, to set at liberty those who are oppressed, to proclaim the acceptable year of the Lord. (Luke 4:16–19)

ACKNOWLEDGMENTS

A SPECIAL THANK you to the priests and Catholics who helped me begin the lifelong process of reorienting my life toward God, in an authentic way, with no secrets (as if I could hide from God anyway).

To my partner, Chris, for challenging me to be the best person I am capable of being. And for recognizing my gifts before seeing my imperfections.

A special thank you to my friends, who endured several difficult years of crisis as I tried to learn how to be more authentic. I am grateful for your patience and your virtues.

With love for my family at Holy Rosary Italian Catholic Church. When I had trouble finding a healthy and safe environment, you provided it. Thank you to moral theologian Fr. Diego Puricelli.

A special thank you to Queen of Peace Catholic Church in Arlington, Virginia. You introduced me to a life of service oriented toward the marginalized. Thank you to Fr. Tim Hickey and Sally Diaz-Wells.

With appreciation for my friends at the Community of Sant'Egidio, including Matthew Stifter and Dani Clark. My friends continue to help me learn how to live the three community pillars of daily life: Prayer, Poor, and Peace.

BIBLIOGRAPHY

Aquinas, St. Thomas. n.d. *Summa Theologica.* Christian Classics Ethereal Library. https://www.ccel.org/ccel/aquinas/summa.FP_Q19_A4.html.

Ball, M. 2014. "No, Liberals Don't Control the Democratic Party." *The Atlantic.* https://www.theatlantic.com/politics/archive/2014/02/no-liberals-dont-control-the-democratic-party/283653/.

Barry, R. 1995. "The Development of the Roman Catholic Teachings on Suicide." *Notre Dame Journal of Law, Ethics & Public Policy*, 9, no. 2: 449. https://scholarship.law.nd.edu/ndjlepp/vol9/iss2/4.

Bianchi, M. 2014. *Questioni di Teologia Morale e Pratica.* EDUCatt Università Cattolica.

Bowman, T. 1989. "Address to the Subcommittee on African American Affairs." United States Conference of Catholic Bishops. https://www.usccb.org/issues-and-action/cultural-diversity/african-american/resources/upload/Transcript-Sr-Thea-Bowman-June-1989-Address.pdf.

Burgis, L. 2021. *Wanting.* St. Martin's Press.

Caldwell, S. 2022. "Cardinal Hollerich: Church Teaching on Gay Sex Is 'False' and Can Be Changed." *Catholic Herald*, February 3. https://catholicherald.co.uk/cardinal-hollerich-church-teaching-on-gay-sex-is-false-and-can-be-changed/.

Calogero, S. 1994. "Meaning and Action: Relating Knowledge and Action in the Thought of St. Thomas Aquinas." PhD dissertation, Loyola University. https://ecommons.luc.edu/luc_diss/3436.

Czerny, M. 2022. "The Renewal of Theology as a Dialogue from Within." *La Civiltà Cattolica*, March 7. https://www.laciviltacattolica.com/the-renewal-of-theology-as-a-dialogue-from-within/.

Czerny, M., and Barone, C. 2023. "Renewing and Realizing the Social Doctrine of the Church." *La Civiltà Cattolica*, May 22. https://www.laciviltacattolica.com/renewing-and-realizing-the-social-doctrine-of-the-church/.

Dell'Anna, C. 2024. Directed by Alejandro Monteverde. *Cabrini*. Angel Studios.

Delpini, M. 2023. Viviamo di una vita ricevuta. September 15. Archdiocese of Milan. https://www.chiesadimilano.it/cms/documenti-del-vescovo/mario-delpini-documenti-del-vescovo/lettera-pastorale/viviamo-di-una-vita-ricevuta-2509094.html.

Di Luccio, P., and Grilli, M. 2019. "Gesù e i farisei." *La Civiltà Cattolica*, September 7. https://www.laciviltacattolica.it/articolo/gesu-e-i-farisei/.

Ehrman, B. 2024. *Triumph of Christianity: How a Forbidden Religion Swept the World*. Simon and Schuster.

Fitzgibbons, R. 2005. "The Psychology behind Homosexual Tendencies. Interviewed by Z. D. Dispatch. Eternal Word Television Network. December 5. https://www.ewtn.com/catholicism/library/psychology-behind-homosexual-tendencies-2944.

Flemish-Speaking Catholic Bishops of Belgium. 2022. "Being Pastorally Close to Homosexuals: For a Welcoming Church That Excludes No One." September. https://www.cathobel.be/wp-content/uploads/2022/09/20220920-PB-Aanspreekpunt-Bijlage-1.pdf.

Francis, Pope. 2017. "Address of His Holiness Pope Francis to Participants in the Meeting Promoted by the Pontifical Council for Promoting the New Evangelization." The Holy See. October 11.

https://www.vatican.va/content/francesco/en/speeches/2017/october/documents/papa-francesco_20171011_convegno-nuova-evangelizzazione.html.

———. 2020. *Fratelli Tutti*. The Holy See. https://www.vatican.va/content/francesco/en/encyclicals/documents/papa-francesco_20201003_enciclica-fratelli-tutti.html.

———. 2021. "Audience with the Faithful of the Diocese of Rome." September 18. https://press.vatican.va/content/salastampa/en/bollettino/pubblico/2021/09/18/210918d.html.

———. 2023. "Full Text: Pope Francis' Letter to New Doctrine Chief Archbishop Fernandez." *Catholic News Agency*. https://www.catholicnewsagency.com/news/254712/full-text-pope-francis-letter-to-new-doctrine-chief-archbishop-fernandez.

———. 2024. "L'Udienza Generale." The Holy See. January 17. https://press.vatican.va/content/salastampa/it/bollettino/pubblico/2024/01/17/0050/00096.html.

Fumagalli, A. 2020. *L'Amore Possibile*. Cittadella Editrice.

———. 2024. "L'amore possibile: persone omosessuali e morale cattolica." *Istituo Teologico*, May 7.

Grech, M. 2014. Speech by Bishop Mario Grech during the III Extraordinary General Assembly of the Synod of Bishops. Archdiocese of Malta. October 8. https://church.mt/speech-by-bishop-mario-grech-during-the-iii-extraordinary-general-assembly-of-the-synod-of-bishops/.

Grillo, A. 2020. "La trasformazione della sessualità come segno dei tempi. Cinque spunti per una riflessione ulteriore—2." Vino Nuovo. November 18. https://www.vinonuovo.it/teologia/etica/la-trasformazione-della-sessualita-come-segno-dei-tempi-cinque-spunti-per-una-riflessione-ulteriore-2/.

———. 2022. *Cattolicesimo e omosessualità*. Editrice Morcelliana.

Guarino, T. 2018. *The Disputed Teachings of Vatican II*. William B. Erdmans Publishing Company.

Hansen, L. 2015. "Cardinal Marx on Francis, the Synod, Women in the Church and Gay Relationships: An Exclusive Interview with the President of the German Bishops' Conference and Papal Adviser." *America Magazine*, January 2022. https://www.americamagazine.org/issue/cardinal-marx-francis-synod-women-church-and-gay-relationships.

Hartnett, D. 2015. "Sensus Fidei: Owning Our 'Sense of the Faithful.'" YouTube. March 16. https://www.youtube.com/watch?v=_iyOp-UNsJQ.

Hawksley, T. 2020. *Peacebuilding and Catholic Social Teaching*. University of Notre Dame Press.

Herzman, R., and Cook, W. 2013. *Francis of Assisi*. The Great Courses. July 8. https://www.thegreatcourses.com/courses/francis-of-assisi.

Honings, B. 1996. "The Man of the New Creation: From the Image of God to the Likeness of Christ. Pontifical Council for Pastoral Assistance to Health Care Workers." In *"In the Image and Likeness of God: Always?" Disturbances of the Human Mind.* Proceedings of the Eleventh International Conference Organized by the Pontificial Council for Pastoral Assistance to Health Care Workers, 46–51. Vatican City. https://www.humandevelopment.va/content/dam/sviluppoumano/pubblicazioni-documenti/archivio/salute/dolentium-hominum-en-1-72/DH_34_En.pdf.

Horan, D. 2019. *Catholicity and Emerging Personhood: A Contemporary Theological Anthropology (Catholicity in an Evolving Universe)*. Orbis Books.

Houdaille, C. 2022. "No One Can Be Denied a Blessing, Says Top Family Official in Rome." *LaCroix International*, November 18. https://international.la-croix.com/news/religion/no-one-can-be-denied-a-blessing-says-top-family-official-in-rome/16925.

Houlihan, P. 2015. *Catholicism and the Great War*. Cambridge University Press.

International Theological Commission. 2011. "Theology Today: Perspectives, Principles, and Criteria." November 29. https://

www.vatican.va/roman_curia/congregations/cfaith/cti_documents/rc_cti_doc_20111129_teologia-oggi_en.html.

Keane, J. T. 2023. "Philosopher for a Secular Age: Charles Taylor's Influence in the Catholic Church." *America Magazine*, March 21. https://www.americamagazine.org/arts-culture/2023/03/21/cbc-column-charles-taylor-244944.

Keenan, J. 2010. *A History of Catholic Moral Theology in the Twentieth Century*. Continuum International Publishing Group.

———. 2022. *A History of Catholic Theological Ethics*. Paulist Press.

———. 2023. "It's Time for a Catholic Ethic That Sees Sexuality as a Gift, Not a Curse." *National Catholic Reporter*, March 28. https://www.ncronline.org/opinion/guest-voices/its-time-catholic-ethic-sees-sexuality-gift-not-curse.

Larkman, C. 2015. "James Nelson, Groundbreaking Ethics and Sexuality Scholar, Dies at 85." *The Christian Century*, November 11. https://www.christiancentury.org/article/2015-10/james-nelson-groundbreaking-ethics-and-sexuality-scholar-dies-85.

Lawler, M., and T. Salzman. 2022. "Catholic Arguments against Homosexual Acts and Relationships: Emotional Revulsion or Rational Argument?" *Sexes* 3, no 4: 564–77. https://doi.org/10.3390/sexes304004.1.

Lefebure, L. D. 1996. "Victims, Violence and the Sacred: The Thought of Rene Girard. (Includes Bibliographies of Books by and about Girard)." *The Christian Century* 113, no. 36: 1226–29.

Manson, J. 2011. "The Church's New Role as a Refuge for Absolutism." *National Catholic Reporter*, February 28. https://www.ncronline.org/blogs/grace-margins/churchs-new-role-refuge-absolutism.

Mastrofini, F. 2022. "Infallibility on Moral Issues?" *Settimana News*, August 19. https://www.settimananews.it/teologia/infallibilita-sulle-questioni-morali/.

McElroy, R. 2023. "Cardinal McElroy Responds to His Critics on Sexual Sin, the Eucharist, and LGBT and Divorced/Remarried

Catholics." *America Magazine*, March 2. https://www.americamagazine.org/faith/2023/03/02/mcelroy-eucharist-sin-inclusion-response-244827.

McElwee, J. 2016. "Francis Asks Priests to Learn That Life Isn't Black and White, but Shades of Grey." *National Catholic Reporter*, August 25. https://www.ncronline.org/news/vatican/francis-asks-seminaries-teach-life-isnt-black-and-white-shades-grey.

Merrigan, T. 2009. "The Imagination in the Life and Thought of John Henry Newman." *Cahiers Victorianes et Édouardiens* 70. https://doi.org/10.4000/cve.4829.

Michel, B., and G. Nopper. 2022. "Chur Bishop Tolerates Blessing of Homosexuals." *Blick*, February 24. https://www.blick.ch/news/urner-rebellenpriester-wendelin-bucheli-67-darf-bleiben-churer-bischof-duldet-segnung-von-homosexuellen-id17267455.html.

Moia, L. 2019. "Omosessualità, quale bene nella relazione?" *Avvenire*, February 19. https://www.avvenire.it/chiesa/pagine/abusi-nella-chiesa-4.

———. 2020. "Il libro. Omosessuali, le risposte necessarie." *Avvenire*, October 14. https://www.avvenire.it/chiesa/pagine/omosessuali-libro-fumagalli-prefazione-semeraro.

———. 2022. "Il cardinale Zuppi: gli omosessuali? La diversità di tutti è ricchezza." *Avvenire*, May 23. https://www.avvenire.it/chiesa/pagine/zuppi-gli-omosessuali-la-diversit-ricchezza.

Moons, J. 2022. "Celebrating Gay Relationships in the Church? What Happened in Belgium and Why It's Good News." *Outreach*, November 7. https://outreach.faith/2022/11/celebrating-gay-relationships-in-the-church-what-happened-in-belgium-and-why-its-good-news/.

Noceti, S. 2016. "Il Sensus Fidelium: Una riflessione ecclesiologica." In *La Morale Ecclesiale Tra Sensus Fidelium E Magistero*, edited by A. Rovello. Cittadella Editrice.

O'Brien, K. 2004. "Jesuit Karl Rahner Was One of the Most Influential Theologians of the 20th Century. But He Was First and Foremost a Priest." *America Magazine*, May 3. https://www.americamagazine.org/faith/2004/05/03/thursdays-rahner.

Petrà, B. 2021. *Una Futura Morale Sessuale Cattolica* 1st ed. Assisi: Cittadella Editrice.

Pew Research Center. 2022. "As Partisan Hostility Grows, Signs of Frustration with the Two-Party System." https://www.pewresearch.org/wp-content/uploads/sites/20/2022/08/PP_2022.09.08_partisan-hostility_REPORT.pdf.

Pius XII, Pope. 1939. *Summi Pontifatus*. The Holy See. October 20. https://www.vatican.va/content/pius-xii/en/encyclicals/documents/hf_p-xii_enc_20101939_summi-pontificatus.html.

———. 1950. *Humani Generis*. August 12. https://www.vatican.va/content/pius-xii/en/encyclicals/documents/hf_p-xii_enc_12081950_humani-generis.html.

Pontifical Biblical Commission. 2019. "Che cosa è l'uomo?" Sal 8,5. The Holy See. https://www.vatican.va/roman_curia/congregations/cfaith/pcb_documents/rc_con_cfaith_doc_20190930_cosa-e-luomo_it.html.

Puricelli, D. 2023. "Homily for the 6th Sunday of Easter." Holy Rosary Italian Catholic Church.

Queen Donnelly, M. 1990. "Sister Thea Bowman (1937–1990)." *America Magazine*. April 28. https://www.americamagazine.org/issue/100/sister-thea-bowman-1937-1990.

Reeves, R. 2015. "World War I and the Church. Gordon-Conwell Theological Seminary." YouTube. July 28. https://www.youtube.com/watch?v=EroeM04JtdI.

Rohr, R. 2022. "Unlocking Us: On Spirituality, Certitude, and Infinite Love, Part 1 of 2." Interview by B. Brown. April 20. https://brenebrown.com/podcast/spirituality-certitude-and-infinite-love-part-1-of-2/.

Rondini, D. 2000. *Communion and Liberation: A Movement in the Church*. Translated by P. Stevenson and S. Scott. McGill-Queen's University Press.

Sacred Congregation for Doctrine of the Faith. 1975. "Persona Humana." *Holy See*. https://www.catholicnewsagency.com/news/254712/full-text-pope-francis-letter-to-new-doctrine-chief-archbishop-fernandez.

Selling, J. 2016. *Reframing Catholic Theological Ethics*. Oxford University Press.

Siker, J. 2023. "Does the Bible Condemn Homosexuality? Guest Interview with Jeffrey Siker." Interview by B. Ehrman. Misquoting Jesus Podcast. March 14. https://www.youtube.com/watch?v=iFYTTG3Q37w.

Spadaro, A. 2018. "'Today the Church Needs to Grow in Discernment: Pope Francis Meets with Polish Jesuits." *La Civilta Cattolica*, December 11. https://www.laciviltacattolica.com/today-the-church-needs-to-grow-in-discernment-pope-francis-meets-with-polish-jesuits/.

———. 2023. "Crisis and the Future of the Church." *La Civiltà Cattolic*, January 11. https://www.laciviltacattolica.com/crisis-and-the-future-of-the-church/.

Tadié, S. 2023. "'Several' French Bishops Ask Pope to Reformulate Catholic Doctrine on Homosexuality." *National Catholic Register*, March 13. https://www.ncregister.com/blog/some-french-bishops-ask-pope-to-reformulate-doctrine.

Taylor, C. 2007. *A Secular Age*. Belknap Press of Harvard University Press.

Tobin, J. 2019. "Pope Francis and the Future of the American Church." Interview by M. Malone. *America*, September 24. YouTube. https://www.youtube.com/watch?v=7SNxo3dEVvY.

Tornielli, A. 2016. "L'evoluzione della dottrina spiegata da «Civiltà Cattolica»." *La Stampa*, April 28. https://www.lastampa.it/vatican-insider/it/2016/04/28/news/l-evoluzione-della

-dottrina-spiegata-da-civilta-cattolica-1.35020142/#google_vignette.

Watkins, D. 2022. “Pope: ‘Family Life and Love Help Moral Theology Interpret Faith.’” *Vatican News*, May 13. https://www.vaticannews.va/en/pope/news/2022-05/pope-francis-moral-theology-conference-amoris-laetitia.html.

White, C. 2018. “Courage Founder Pushed Bishops to Resist Zero Tolerance on Abuse.” *Crux*, October 8. https://cruxnow.com/church-in-the-usa/2018/10/courage-founder-pushed-bishops-to-resist-zero-tolerance-on-abuse.

Wooden, C. 2015. “Stable Gay Relationship Is Better Than a ‘Temporary’ One, Says Cardinal Schönborn.” *Catholic Herald*, September 11. https://catholicherald.co.uk/stable-gay-relationship-is-better-than-a-temporary-one-says-cardinal-schonborn/.